How You

Can Become

a

Strong

Christian

DAG HEWARD-MILLS

Parchment House

First published 2015 by Parchment House
16th Printing 2021

Find out more about Dag Heward-Mills at:

Healing Jesus Campaign
Email: evangelist@daghewardmills.org
Website: www.daghewardmills.org
Facebook: Dag Heward-Mills
Twitter: ' @EvangelistDag

ISBN : 978-1-61395-519-2

Contents

CHAPTER 1

What It Means to be a Strong Christian

Finally, my brethren, BE STRONG IN THE LORD, and in the power of his might.

Ephesians 6:10

All through the Bible, Christians are exhorted to be strong. You will see the phrase, 'be strong' appearing many times throughout the Bible. In order to be strong you must strengthen yourself. Most Christians are strong in their bodies, strong in politics, strong in academics, strong in business, strong in relationships but not strong in the Lord. God is emphasizing that you must be strong in the Lord.

To be strong in the Lord is to be a strong Christian. Many people come to know the Lord but never become strong in the Lord. They remain spiritual weaklings for the rest of their lives. This book will teach you how to become a good and strong Christian. There are a number of things that characterize a good strong Christian. You must aim to develop all these attributes if you are going to be a good strong believer. To be a strong Christian you must develop spirituality, zeal, maturity, holiness and steadfastness in the Lord.

There are several different areas of your life that must be developed if you are to ever be called a strong Christian. This whole book is about developing these areas that turn you into a strong Christian. The nine areas you need to develop if you want to be strong in the Lord are listed below.

1. To be a strong Christian is to develop a deeper Christian life.

   Deep calleth unto deep at the noise of thy waterspouts: all thy waves and thy billows are gone over me.

                                                                    Psalm 42:7

2. To be a strong Christian is to become steadfast.

   Therefore, my beloved brethren, be ye stedfast, unmoveable, always abounding in the work of the Lord, forasmuch as ye know that your labour is not in vain in the Lord.

                                                            1 Corinthians 15:58

3. To be a strong Christian is to become unmoveable.

    Therefore, my beloved brethren, be ye stedfast, unmoveable, always abounding in the work of the Lord, forasmuch as ye know that your labour is not in vain in the Lord.

    1 Corinthians 15:58

4. To be a strong Christian is to become spiritual.

    And I, brethren, could not speak unto you as unto spiritual, but as unto carnal, even as unto babes in Christ.

    1 Corinthians 3:1

5. To be a strong Christian is to become holy.

    Follow peace with all men, and holiness, without which no man shall see the Lord.

    Hebrews 12:14

6. To be a strong Christian is to become mature.

    That we henceforth be no more children, tossed to and fro, and carried about with every wind of doctrine, by the sleight of men, and cunning craftiness, whereby they lie in wait to deceive.

    Ephesians 4:14

7. To be a strong Christian is to be zealously affected always in a good thing. To be strong in the Lord is to be full of zeal.

    But it is good to be zealously affected always in a good thing, and not only when I am present with you.

    Galatians 4:18

8. To be a strong Christian is to become fruitful.

    Ye have not chosen me, but I have chosen you, and ordained you, that ye should go and BRING FORTH FRUIT, and that your fruit should remain: that

whatsoever ye shall ask of the Father in my name, he may give it you.

John 15:16

9. To be a strong Christian is to be in a state of readiness to meet God at any time.

Therefore thus will I do unto thee, O Israel: and because I will do this unto thee, prepare to meet thy God, O Israel.

Amos 4:12

Six Reasons Why You Must Strengthen Yourself

1. **Strengthen yourself so that you can overcome the wicked one.**

   I have written unto you, fathers, because ye have known him that is from the beginning. I have written unto you, young men, BECAUSE YE ARE STRONG, and the word of God abideth in you, AND YE HAVE OVERCOME THE WICKED ONE.

1 John 2:14

The wicked one is not a weakling. It is only when you are strong that you can overcome the wicked one. If you joke with the enemy, you will have yourself to blame. Fighting Satan is to fight a seasoned warrior who has seen many battles. The devil has fought many Christians over the years. He is experienced in destroying and tempting Christians. The devil was alive when Jesus was alive. He is not a newcomer, but you are! Rise up and become stronger so that you will defeat the wicked one.

When I was in secondary school, I was bullied by wicked seniors. I went through all sorts of torture and punishment inflicted on me by people who were just a year ahead of me. During this time, I realised the depth of wickedness that existed in the heart of mankind. These thirteen and fourteen year old boys exercised ultimate power over me because they happened to be a year ahead.

Sometimes, I was asked to do what they called the 'monkey dance.' At other times I was asked to do the 'Tower of Liberty' punishment. Sometimes, I had to scrub toilets and showers till 3.00am. Sometimes I had to carry several buckets of manure over a distance of five kilometres. Sometimes I was asked to stand guard and kill any mosquitoes that flew around the bed. Other punishments which existed included eating *gari* (cassava flakes) and mashed bitter quinine tablets. For several months, I suffered under the hands of these wicked seniors. One day, I noticed that one of my classmates was never called, never sent anywhere, never harassed and never punished! But I knew why! He was far bigger and stronger than the seniors! This classmate of mine was bigger, stronger and older than the rest of my class and the seniors were genuinely afraid of him. He could have beaten up any of them up at a moment's notice.

There were times the seniors would shout out: "*One small boy!*" This meant that all juniors had to run towards the senior who had called for "*One small boy!*" We would all run but the older, bigger stronger boy would utterly ignore the seniors and carry on doing what he was doing. No one dared ask him anything. They were scared of him because he was so strong! But I was not strong. I was weak, beatable and punishable. I was a good prey for those wicked heartless seniors. If only I could be as strong as my big and muscular classmate.

This is where I learnt the importance of strength! When you are strong, the wicked ones are forced to leave you alone. The wicked ones know that they will be defeated. Satan will not dare to even start a problem because he knows it will not end well for him. You must be strong because when something stronger than you comes against you, it will overcome you and destroy you.

When a strong man armed keepeth his palace, his goods are in peace: but when a stronger than he shall come upon him, and overcome him, he taketh from him all his armour wherein he trusted, and divideth his spoils.

Luke 11:21-22

This should be the greatest motivation for strengthening yourself! As you become stronger, the wicked one is forced to leave you alone because he knows that many temptations will simply not work on you. Be strong in the Lord!

2.   **You must strengthen yourself in the Lord because your enemy is planning to attack you again.**

And they slew every one his man: and the Syrians fled; and Israel pursued them: and Benhadad the king of Syria escaped on an horse with the horsemen.
And the king of Israel went out, and smote the horses and chariots, and slew the Syrians with a great slaughter.
And the prophet came to the king of Israel, and said unto him, GO, STRENGTHEN THYSELF, and mark, and see what thou doest: for at the return of the year the king of Syria will come up against thee.

1 Kings 20:20-22

Your enemy is planning an attack. Whether you like it or not you will be attacked. The enemy has eyed you and selected you as a prime target. Without provocation the enemy will strike when his season comes. Jesus was attacked over and over throughout His life and ministry. Even on the cross, in His very last few minutes, Jesus experienced unrelenting temptations and attacks. I want you to decide to become the strongest Christian possible because you are going to defeat the enemy many times over.

3.   **Strengthen yourself so you can run your race properly.**

Their line is gone out through all the earth, and their words to the end of the world. In them hath he set a

tabernacle for the sun, which is as a bridegroom coming out of his chamber, and rejoiceth AS A STRONG MAN TO RUN A RACE.

Psalms 19:4-5

You will notice that athletes, even women, are very muscular and strong. Without strength you cannot run a race. You need to strengthen yourself if you are going to be a spiritual athlete and run your course. All of us are involved in the Christian race. We must run the race that is set before us and we must win. "Wherefore seeing we also are compassed about with so great a cloud of witnesses, let us lay aside every weight, and the sin which doth so easily beset us, and let us run with patience the race that is set before us," (Hebrews 12:1).

4. Strengthen yourself so that you can withstand in the evil day.

Wherefore take unto you the whole armour of God, that ye may be able to withstand in the evil day, and having done all, to stand.

Ephesians 6:13

Everybody reacts differently in the day of a crisis. Some people, with soft hearts, collapse and die in the day of a crisis. Others go mad in the day of a crisis. You see, in the day of your crisis everything changes. Without strength, the pressure, the crises and the problems will destroy you. It is time to be strong in the Lord so that you can withstand in the evil day. There are others who have experienced so many crises in their lives and are still standing. Will you be left standing in the evil day or will you fall and give up when the pressure rises? It is time to prepare yourself for the day of crisis and pressure.

Those who plan to merely pass an exam often fail. When something goes wrong, they are quickly tipped into the fail zone. That is why you must aim higher so that if something goes wrong, you do not fall below the mark. Decide to be far stronger than you really need to be. In the evil day, you will be well able to withstand the pressure.

5. Strengthen yourself so that you can help other people.

We then that are strong ought to bear the infirmities of the weak, and not to please ourselves.

Romans 15:1

When you are on an aeroplane, they teach you to put on your oxygen masks in the event of an emergency. They also ask that parents should put on their own oxygen masks first before attempting to help their children. Why is this? Should they not attend to the children first since they are weaker? Answer is 'No'! The parents will need oxygen to keep them alive and strong. If they are not alive and strong, they will not be able to help anyone, not even their own children. Strength is important if you are going to help your neighbour. Have you ever wondered why countries like Senegal, Guinea or Ghana are not asked for financial or military assistance when there is a world crisis? People often look to America because they are well known for their financial and military strength.

Without strength you cannot bear the infirmities of the weak. There is no way you can help other people if you yourself are down and out. God has called you to be strong in him and to become a blessing to other people. Develop strength so that you can be a blessing to many other people.

6. Strengthen yourself because it is a wise thing to be strong.

A WISE MAN IS STRONG; yea, a man of knowledge increaseth strength.

Proverbs 24:5

Since the Second World War, most nations have strengthened themselves because they have learnt from experience that it is wise to develop strength lest another tyrant like Hitler should arise in their midst. The end result is that Europe has become an armed nuclear camp waiting to be ignited.

Indeed, European nations prefer to arm themselves than to sit down in weakness, lest anyone rise up to create another war. You must not sit down in weakness. The devil will take advantage of you as soon as he realises you are not wise enough to prepare yourself in times of peace. You must strengthen yourself because it is a wise thing to do.

CHAPTER 2

How to Have a Deeper Christian Life

Deep calleth unto deep ...

Psalm 42:7

1. Develop deep roots in the Lord.

They on the rock are they, which, when they hear, receive the word with joy; and THESE HAVE NO ROOT, which for a while believe, and in time of temptation fall away.

Luke 8:13

The parable of the sower gives various reasons why some of the seeds could not grow. Some seeds could not grow because they fell on rocky soil. Jesus explained that these are the ones who receive the Word of God with joy, and even believe for a while. But in the time of testing, they fall away because they have no root.

A time of testing will surely come for every Christian. If you are *shallow*, in the time of testing, you *will* fall. Through experience I have noticed that many Christians do not have deep roots. They do not know God for themselves. They cannot even explain why they do the things they do. They don't know why they belong to a particular church. They do not know why they speak in tongues. They do not even know why they give offerings. When they face a little criticism, they get confused and have no defence.

Having no personal experience with God, these are the people who can never say, "God spoke to me." They have no convictions of their own. A close friend who brought me up in the Lord deviated from Christianity, and became a member of a cult. But I did not follow him into that cult because I had my own deep-rooted convictions. I know why I am serving the Lord, and so my father, mother or closest friend cannot change my mind. Many Christians who are not rooted in sound biblical doctrine can easily be persuaded to follow fables. Some born-again believers fall away because they do not know the difference between the true gospel, and the beliefs of sects like the Jehovah Witnesses.

Once, I was standing in the city of Accra when a Jehovah's Witness came up to me to try to convert me to his faith.

11

He asked, "Do you believe in the Holy Spirit?"

I replied, "I certainly do!"

Then I asked him, "Have *you* heard of 'speaking in tongues'?"

He said, "Yes. But I don't believe in it."

So I asked him, "What is *this*...?"

Then I released a string of tongues in the direction of this sincere (but sincerely wrong) gentleman.

This ended our conversation. He fled! If I were not convinced that speaking in tongues was an ability that came with the Holy Spirit, he could have confused me. But I knew my Bible, and I knew (as I still do today) that the Holy Spirit is from God, and speaking in tongues is one of His gifts.

Don't just speak in tongues because others are speaking in tongues. You must know why tongues sound like a monotonous and repetitive language. It is because the Bible says, "with a stammering tongue will I speak to you". Tongues are described as a stammering tongue. It is not just an ordinary language. It is a heavenly language that comes out in a stammering fashion.

You may be in a church, but if you are not "*deep*" you will fall away at the next shaking and crisis. Next time there is a problem in the church, your membership and commitment will be shaken. Only a "shallow" Christian would fall away when a great man of God gets into some scandalous sin. What have the sins of that man of God got to do with your own salvation? Why on earth would you think of leaving Christ because of your pastor's mistakes? Christians behave in this way because they themselves are shallow!

I am the pastor of a large church. I know many people would do anything I tell them to. But I always tell my church members not to follow me if I do not follow Christ. After all, I am also a man, and can make mistakes. I tell them, "If I tell you to do something that is not biblical, do not do it. Only do things which can be supported by the Bible."

If you are not sure about anything your pastor is saying, just ask him, "Please Sir, what is the scriptural basis for this new revelation?"

Not abiding by this principle is the reason why some so-called ministers are able to dupe people out of all their earthly possessions. This is because the pastors know that they are dealing with shallow people. Paul said, "Follow me as long as I follow Christ". He was a man subject to like passions, so whatever he did had to be scrutinized by the book of books: the Bible!

Did you know that Aaron led the people of Israel to build a golden calf after God had delivered them from Egypt? These people were saved all right, but were shallow in their experience with God. When Moses was held up on the mountain, the Israelites in their shallow faith, turned shortly to idols and declared, "These be thy gods, O Israel, which brought thee up out of the land of Egypt."

Don't be shallow and light, blown about by every wind of doctrine! Don't just follow the crowd! It is shallow people who just follow the crowd. Many became calf worshippers in the days of Aaron because they followed the crowd. Many murmured and were destroyed in the days of Moses and the ten spies because they followed the crowd. Many got involved in the killing of Jesus, the Son of God because they followed the crowd.

Following the crowd can be dangerous! Don't be a shallow Christian. Be deep. Don't be a believer for just a while. Let your roots grow deep. As the songwriter says, "*Draw me deeper, Lord!*"

2. Be filled! Be filled! Be filled!

There are many Christians who are empty. There is nothing in them. They have little or no Word in them, neither are they full of the Holy Spirit or of love. They may speak in tongues, but the Bible says whenever they do so, they are just making a lot of noise.

Emptiness will attract other things to fill that empty space.

A spiritual vacuum will be filled with spiritual things, either positively or negatively. Nature abhors a vacuum, and every space will be filled.

And when he [an evil spirit] cometh, he findeth it UNOCCUPIED...
Luke 11:25 (Goodspeed Translation)

Empty Christians are targets for the enemy. The devil will try to fill you with evil tendencies because of the emptiness within you.

Seven Things You Must Be Filled With

1. Be filled with the fullness of God.

And to know the love of Christ, which passeth knowledge, that ye might be FILLED WITH ALL THE FULNESS OF GOD.

Ephesians 3:19

2. Be filled with the Spirit.

Do not get drunk on wine, which leads to debauchery. Instead, BE FILLED WITH THE SPIRIT.

Ephesians 5:18

3. Be filled with the knowledge of His will.

For this reason, since the day we heard about you, we have not stopped praying for you and asking God to FILL YOU WITH THE KNOWLEDGE OF HIS WILL through all spiritual wisdom and understanding.

Colossians 1:9

4. Be filled with joy.

Greatly desiring to see thee, being mindful of thy tears, that I may be FILLED WITH JOY;

2 Timothy 1:4

5. Be filled with faith.

And the saying pleased the whole multitude: and they chose Stephen, a man FULL OF FAITH and of the Holy Ghost, and Philip, and Prochorus, and Nicanor, and Timon, and Parmenas, and Nicolas a proselyte of Antioch:

Acts 6:5

6. Be filled with all knowledge.

And I myself also am persuaded of you, my brethren, that ye also are full of goodness, FILLED WITH ALL KNOWLEDGE, able also to admonish one another.

Romans 15:14

7. Be filled with goodness.

And I myself also am persuaded of you, my brethren, that ye also are FULL OF GOODNESS, filled with all knowledge, able also to admonish one another.

Romans 15:14

Stephen was full of something positive. He was full of faith and the Holy Ghost. That is why he went on to become a great evangelist.

What are you filling your spirit with? Fill your spirit with the Word of God, with faith, with good Christian music. Do not mess around with non-Christian music; it will fill your mind with junk! Fill your time with church activities. If you don't fill your life with these good things *something else* will fill it. Drive away the emptiness from your spiritual life. This is a fundamental key to becoming a strong Christian.

If you are not filled with good things, you will begin to be filled with negative things. There are several evil things that you can be filled with. Do not take it lightly. Nature abhors a vacuum. If you are not filled with the good things you will be filled with the evil things that the Bible teaches about.

Seven Things You Must Not Be Filled With

1. Do not be filled with unrighteousness.

Being filled with all UNRIGHTEOUSNESS, fornication, wickedness, covetousness, maliciousness; full of envy, murder, debate, deceit, malignity; whisperers.

Romans 1:29

2. Do not be filled with fornication.

Being filled with all unrighteousness, FORNICATION, wickedness, covetousness, maliciousness; full of envy, murder, debate, deceit, malignity; whisperers.

Romans 1:29

3. Do not be filled with wickedness and maliciousness.

Being filled with all unrighteousness, fornication, WICKEDNESS, covetousness, MALICIOUSNESS; full of envy, murder, debate, deceit, malignity; whisperers.

Romans 1:29

4. Do not be filled with covetousness.

Being filled with all unrighteousness, fornication, wickedness, COVETOUSNESS, maliciousness; full of envy, murder, debate, deceit, malignity; whisperers.

Romans 1:29

5. Do not be filled with envy and murder .

Being filled with all unrighteousness, fornication, wickedness, covetousness, maliciousness; full of ENVY, MURDER, debate, deceit, malignity; whisperers.

Romans 1:29

6. Do not be filled with deceit.

Being filled with all unrighteousness, fornication, wickedness, covetousness, maliciousness; full of envy, murder, debate, DECEIT, malignity; whisperers.

Romans 1:29

7. Do not be full of cursing and bitterness.

Whose mouth is FULL OF CURSING AND BITTERNESS.

Romans 3:14

CHAPTER 3

How to Be a Steadfast Christian

Therefore, my beloved brethren, BE YE STEDFAST, unmoveable, always abounding in the work of the Lord, forasmuch as ye know that your labour is not in vain in the Lord.

1 Corinthians 15:58

Steadfastness is an important word that was developed by the navy. Ships on the sea really needed to have the ability to stay on course because their lives depended on it. The sea is so vast and there was only a limited amount of food on a ship. If you took the wrong direction, you could go for several days and simply arrive in the middle of nowhere in danger of dying from thirst and starvation.

Think about it. In the days when there was no electricity and no radio communication, it would be extremely important to be able to stay on course. Imagine that you had five sheep, six pigs and thirty chickens on board. Imagine that you had ten sacks of rice, four sacks of onions, five sacks of tomatoes, and three sacks of oranges. Imagine that you had two barrels of cooking oil and forty barrels of water. Imagine that you had eighty passengers that you had to look after and feed every day whilst you were on the sea. With eighty people eating three times a day, you better be sure you are on the right path to the right place. If you miss your way, you will end up on the open sea with no food and water. Eighty people will eat one pig a day or ten chickens a day. At this rate, all the meat on board would be finished in fourteen days. Also, the eighty people would drink a barrel of water a day and use three barrels every day for bathing and cooking. The water would therefore last for ten days. As you can see, if the captain did not stay in the right direction, they could end up in the middle of the sea after twenty days and still need another fourteen days to find land. It was very important that you were in the hands of someone who was truly *steadfast.*

As you can see, steadfastness was a very important characteristic that seamen had to develop. Steadfastness speaks of the ability to stay in the right direction. It also means you have the ability to come back to the right path when you have strayed away.

It is not only important for ships to develop steadfastness but for born again Christians and even pastors to develop the art of staying steadily on the right path. Indeed, you must develop the art of coming back to the correct path when you have strayed away. These are the keys to developing steadfastness and steadiness in your Christian walk.

1. Develop steadfastness by not *loving* the world.

For Demas hath forsaken me, having LOVED this present world...

2 Timothy 4:10

Demas loved the world. That is why he deserted Paul. If you love somebody, you will eventually gravitate towards that person. This explains why young ladies will leave their loving parents and marry virtual strangers. Love or lust is one of the reasons for that gravitational pull. If you love the world – its money, its women, its men, its glitter – you will find yourself gravitating towards these things. It is therefore important that the Christian should not have any strange love in his heart.

The prodigal son had a strong desire for the world. He wanted to leave home so he could have the pleasures of the world. He was deceived and wanted something else. But there was nothing else! He soon found out that the situation out there was not as good as it was at home.

Often Christians feel they are missing out on something in the world. Sometimes they feel they are losing out on money, sex, glamour and so on. Apart from the love of Christ, if you have any other love in you, you need to be careful of it. If you have any strange lusts in you, you must kill them now, or they will grow up and take over your life.

I once saw a baby snake in my garden. It looked very much like an ordinary worm but it was definitely a snake. So I said to myself, "If I don't kill it now, one day it could kill me." I thought, "It is too dangerous to leave this thing alive. Let me kill it now," I decided. That is how we must deal with some of those loves, lusts and desires lurking within us. Deal with them like I dealt with that snake. Kill them now, when they are small and harmless. If you allow them to grow and to develop, they will destroy you one day.

2. Develop steadfastness by not *lusting* after the things in this world.

> ...and the LUSTS of other things entering in, choke the word, and it becometh unfruitful.
>
> **Mark 4:19**

Lust for anything apart from God's Word is dangerous. It can ruin your life because you will sacrifice so many things to get what you want. There are Christians who will sacrifice anything to ride in a Mercedes Benz. They will steal, cheat and lie to own one. Such believers have a strong desire to have some material possession, and they will do all they can to have it. This strong overpowering desire is what God calls lust. But lust is dangerous! It destroys.

> ... having escaped the corruption that is in the world through lust.
>
> **2 Peter 1:4**

Corruption has come into the world through lust. The spoiling of your life will come through your lusts. The destroying of your happiness will come through your lusts. There are many Christian ladies who have such strong desires to marry that they will sacrifice all principles and all the rules in order to get married. To lust after something is to have a strong, excessive desire for something. Usually it is an uncontrollable, sometimes obsessive desire for a particular thing. One dictionary calls 'lust' an animal desire. Be wary of all forms of lust, whether it's financial lust, sexual lust or power lust. Lust corrupts and destroys good things.

Governments are destroyed and corrupted through their lusts. Governments are often corrupt because of officials who have strong desires to acquire certain possessions. These officials take bribes in exchange for illegal favours. They also receive gifts and handouts in exchange for signing bogus contracts that ruin the economies of entire nations. Lust (strong desires) corrupts people, governments and nations.

3. Develop steadfastness by having a proper fear of judgment.

For we must all appear before the judgment seat of Christ; that every one may receive the things done in his body, according to that he hath done, whether it be good or bad. KNOWING THEREFORE THE TERROR OF THE LORD, WE PERSUADE MEN...

2 Corinthians 5:10-11

In school, I noticed two types of students. There were those who were always conscious of the looming examinations. Others were carefree and unconcerned about upcoming tests. It is those who had a proper fear of examination who did well in school. When you have no fear of judgment or examinations, you live anyhow and stray from the path of righteousness. It is important to have a proper fear of God's judgment so that you will be steadfast and unmoveable from the path of life.

I have heard Christians say that God will never punish them. They quote, "For God so loved the world...". They argue that since God loves the world so much He will not destroy them. They say, "I know God will forgive me." Because of this they add sin to sin without batting an eyelid. God's nature is like two sides of a coin. One side of the coin shows the head, and the other side shows the tail. One side of God's character shows His great love, and the other side shows His judgment.

A Christian sister spoke of a woman who was having an affair with her best friend's husband. Because the two ladies were good friends they would often speak on the phone. Every time this adulteress put the phone down, she would sigh and say, "O God, forgive me for what I'm doing." Strangely, she continued having the affair with her friend's husband. Some people feel that God will not punish them. That is why they continue in sin.

When God shows you one side of His character you will see love, forgiveness and mercy of the highest order. God will forgive and forget your sins. But a time will come when God will show you the other side of His nature; which is judgment, justice, fairness, equity and jurisprudence. These are the two sides of God's nature. We are now in the dispensation of grace. God is showing you mercy and love. Think about all the wicked sins you have committed, but still receive His forgiveness. At a certain point, the Spirit of the Lord will not strive with man anymore. God has to judge you; otherwise there will be chaos in the Kingdom.

The king by judgment establisheth the land...
Proverbs 29:4

God loves you so much that He will punish you when He has to.

4.   Develop steadfastness by not being over-confident.

An over-confident person is someone who has too much trust in his abilities. It is dangerous to be over-confident as a Christian. Being too confident in your righteousness and in your own spirituality is a bad sign.

...Let him that THINKETH HE STANDETH take heed lest he fall.
1 Corinthians 10:12

If you regard yourself or your position in Christ as foolproof, you are in danger of straying from the right path. I have heard some Christians boast about their abilities. This is over-confidence. It reminds me of a particular brother in my church who would regularly come to me and say: "Pastor, your church is so good; I will never leave Lighthouse Chapel." He spoke about his commitment to me and to the church with such conviction. A few months later, he walked out of the church and never returned.

When a Christian continues to boast about his strength, Satan hears him and decides to test him. Where you are over-confident is where you can be the weakest, because you have dropped your guard.

23

You can also tell that a Christian is over-confident by the way he talks about the weaknesses of others. I have heard Christians criticize others as though they could never make the same mistakes. They overestimate their own ability, and look down on others. You need to be humble; otherwise one day you will find yourself in the same shoes, much to your own surprise. Staying on the right track is largely by the grace of God, and not by your own strength.

When David heard that Saul was dead, he didn't ridicule him or rejoice over his death. David could have lashed out at Saul and criticized him at that time. He could have taken the opportunity to talk about how Saul had been disobedient and stubborn. He could have discussed what led to Saul's downfall. Instead he declared,

Tell it not in Gath, publish it not in the streets of Askelon...

2 Samuel 1:20

Although David did not have a problem with stubbornness and disobedience, he did not venture to denounce his predecessor because of his weaknesses. We must all learn something from this example. Let him that thinketh he standeth take heed lest he fall!

5. Develop steadfastness by not being hard and stubborn.

Better is a poor and a wise child than an old and foolish king, who will no more be admonished.

Ecclesiastes 4:13

If you know a stubborn Christian who does not heed to counsel, you are looking at someone who can stray from the paths of righteousness. I have counselled many Christians who never change their lifestyles in spite of all that is said to them. They are bent on doing their own thing. Everybody needs advice. The Bible says there is safety in the multitude of counsel.

I remember counselling a young lady not to continue in a certain unhealthy relationship. I asked, "What makes you different from the other girls he has thrown away? He has had 17 girlfriends, and you are the 18th. The only difference between you and the others is that you are new to him. But one day you will become 'old' just like the others. And he will then throw you away." But she continued to follow the love of her life!

Is there anybody who was mightily blessed by God although he was stubborn and rebellious? Never! Stubbornness to God, to His Word, to His pastors and to biblical counsel is a sign that you will stray away from the right path.

6. Develop steadfastness by not looking back at the world.

To be steadfast you must learn never to look back. In Genesis 19, we can study the testimony of Lot and his wife. Two angels were sent to Lot and his family in Sodom and Gomorrah. Their message was simple:

...Escape for thy life, LOOK NOT BEHIND THEE... lest thou be consumed.
Genesis 19:17

But the Bible declares that Lot's wife looked back and became a pillar of salt. Jesus also reminds us of the terrible mistake that Lot's wife made as she was escaping from Sodom and Gomorrah. She was the only member of the family who looked back at her past. We can liken this to believers who backslid because they kept looking back at the world and all it had to offer. As born-again believers, God has delivered all of us from sin, and it is important that we do not look back.

I always remember the story of a lady who stood before a Christian group to testify. She happily recounted what she had done as an unbeliever:

"I used to go out with many men. They would pick me up to party with me at nightclubs and discos. I danced all night with them. It was great." She said.

With great excitement in her voice, she told the Christians: "I travelled all over the world with them. We really had a good time."

Then her voice dropped and she sadly said, "But I got saved, and here I am in church."

To her, salvation was rather the "bad" thing that happened to her. It was as though being saved was an unfortunate experience. This woman was looking back to the expensive cars, the expensive restaurants and the "good" times she had had as an unbeliever. If you keep on thinking and remembering your past sinful life with nostalgia, you will turn into "a pillar of salt"!

I am looking ahead, and I intend to go forward with God's work. As a medical doctor in full-time ministry, I could look back and consider becoming a professor. There are times when I think it would be nice to develop myself in the medical field. But I am not looking back to my medical profession. I am going forward, preaching, teaching and planting churches all over the world. I have no intention of going back.

If there is a longing in your heart to go backwards or to look backwards, come before the Lord and ask Him to help you "kill" that interest in the past. Let it die! Be steadfast, unmoveable, always abounding in the work of the Lord!

7. Develop steadfastness by allowing yourself to be corrected.

Reprove not a scorner, lest he hate thee: rebuke a wise man, and he will love thee.

Proverbs 9:8

Constant correction will keep you steadily on the path of righteousness. We have come to Christ to learn new things and have a better life. You must be open for correction in every aspect of your life. Every aspect of your life is linked to the other. This is why you need correction in almost every area of your life. God will raise up pastors who will correct you in every area of your life. Please do not be angry when you are corrected in your behaviour, your domestic life, your spiritual life and your school life.

Any believer who gets angry at correction must be watched closely. A wise man will be happy at correction because he will think through it and realize that he is being helped. Often the truth is painful. When Jesus told the crowd in John 8:44 "Ye are of your father the devil..." they were offended.

On one occasion, Jesus addressed Peter and said to him, "Get thee behind me, Satan." Notice that Peter was not angry at being called Satan. After this rebuke, Peter went on to become the great man of God who preached to thousands!

A friend at school told someone who was irritating him, "Satan, get thee behind me." This person was astonished, amazed and very offended at being called "Satan". His reaction was very different from Peter's! I have never referred to anybody as Satan (although I have seen many people behave just like the devil). I wonder what would happen if I dared to correct someone by referring to him as Satan? He would probably explode in anger!

During a visit to one of my branch churches, an instrumentalist was very rude to his choir director. The pastor in charge sternly rebuked this musician. I watched this scene quietly from the side, wondering what would happen next. Fortunately this musician did not get angry at his pastor's rebuke and is still doing well. I know some musicians who would have walked out at that kind of correction.

Better is a poor and a wise child than an old and foolish king, who will no more be admonished.

Ecclesiastes 4:13

God gave us fathers and mothers to correct and advise us. You should thank God if your parents are alive. There are many people who do not have strong fathers to guide them. Such people often go astray. My wife tells me that she wanted to be a secretary for the wrong reasons, but her father counselled her. He encouraged her to study law. Today she is glad that she followed her father's advice and became a lawyer. Those who do not have good parents to guide and correct them are at a disadvantage. Correction will help you stay on track so do not be angry at correction!

CHAPTER 4

How to Be an
Unmoveable Christian

If ye continue in the faith grounded and settled, and BE NOT MOVED AWAY FROM THE HOPE OF THE GOSPEL, which ye have heard, and which was preached to every creature which is under heaven; whereof I Paul am made a minister.

Colossians 1:23

Many Christians are moved away from their original beliefs. A pastor once said to me, 'I have moved away from preaching the true gospel.' He marvelled, 'I don't understand how I got to this place. I do not preach about the cross of Jesus Christ, the blood of Jesus or about the love of God. What I preach is in the Bible. It is close to the truth and parallel to the real gospel. I do not understand how I got here,' he wondered.

Sometimes, when I review my books, I try to see if I have moved away from the things which I originally believed. I am always glad when I find that I still believe most of the things I believed at the beginning. You can trust what I am saying. Many people start out in a certain way but are moved from their original faith. That is why Paul was happy to announce three important things at the end of his life. 'I have kept the faith! I have finished my course! I have run my race!'

Paul experienced a lot of pressure, problems and afflictions during his preaching life. Even when his life was threatened, he said, 'But none of these things move me, neither count I my life dear unto myself, so that I might finish my course with joy, and the ministry, which I have received of the Lord Jesus, to testify the gospel of the grace of God' (Acts 20:24).

1. Do not be moved by offences and afflictions.

That **NO MAN SHOULD BE MOVED BY THESE AFFLICTIONS: for yourselves know that we are appointed thereunto...**

1 Thessalonians 3:3

There are many troubles, afflictions and offenses that you must expect because you are a Christian. It is part of the Christian life. Becoming a Christian is not the same as joining a perfect group of angels. When you join a church you are not joining a group of angels. Decide to be loving and accommodating towards other Christians. Others will also have to put up with you.

I remember one absentee church member whom we visited. We wanted to know why she was not in church anymore. She told us that once, when she came in late, the ushers wrongly seated her and later relocated her. This had happened more than once. So she became offended and decided not to come to church anymore. This person was offended by the inexperienced usher and simply left the church. Imagine that!

Some church members are irritated because the pastor does not seem to remember their names. Others are offended because the pastor did not say hello when he met them in town. Think about this for a moment; why would the pastor deliberately not say hello to his own church member? Does it make sense? Is he trying to gather people or to scatter and offend them? Could it not be that the pastor didn't recognize you, or that he genuinely did not notice you? Think about it!

If you marry a touchy person, you will always have problems. They are the ones who complain, "Why didn't you smile today? I put my toothbrush in the centre, why have you moved it to the right? How come the towel is wet? Don't leave my towel on the bed. Why have you put my shoes here instead of there?" It's very difficult to live with people like that. They are not only difficult marriage partners, but also difficult church members for the pastor. They can even become offended with God Himself!

If I were to be easily offended, I would not have been able to continue in the ministry. Some years ago, I travelled from Ghana to start a church in Zurich. While I was fasting and praying to establish God's work, my father died back home in Ghana.

Throughout the week before he died, he had been seriously ill, but I wasn't fully informed about what was going on. Then one day after I had been praying and fasting for 5 days and nights, my father died about 11 o'clock in the morning. One of my associate pastors called to inform me about what had happened. I was shocked and surprised. And when I put the phone down, I wept like a baby.

I had every reason to be offended with God. Wasn't I on the mission field, doing His work? I consoled myself that I would understand it better by and by and truly, I have not become disillusioned with the ministry. I am pressing on! If a Christian easily gets hurt, he cannot be described as unmoveable.

2. Do not let bitterness move you away from God.

Looking diligently lest any man fail of the grace of God; LEST ANY ROOT OF BITTERNESS SPRINGING UP TROUBLE YOU, and thereby many be defiled.

Hebrews 12:15

Bitterness is an advanced and developed form of offense. Bitterness is deep-seated long-standing complicated offense. Many people who walk out of a church are offended Christians who became bitter. They were probably genuinely offended, and their wounds never healed.

When my wife was pregnant with our second son, Joshua, I sometimes went with her to the antenatal clinic. To while away the time I engaged in conversation with one of the doctors. One morning as I chatted with this doctor, I noticed that one of his toes was missing.

So I asked, "What happened to your toe?"

He answered, "I am a diabetic patient, and I once had an injury to that toe. (You know, the wounds of some diabetic patients don't easily heal)."

He continued, "I hit my toe on an object, but after some time the wound did not heal. This wound deteriorated until it affected my whole leg."

He lamented about how the doctors had even considered amputating his whole leg. However, in the end they decided to cut off only the toe in question. "It was a very traumatic experience for me. That's how I ended up without a toe," he concluded.

As I mused over the story of this missing toe, the Spirit of God spoke to me and said, "This is what happens to Christians who get hurt and never fully recover from their hurts." The Holy Spirit showed me how many Christians and pastors allow their hurts to degenerate into unhealed, gangrenous wounds of the heart. He continued, "They separate themselves from other Christians in the name of being cautious and not wanting to be hurt all over again. This separation eventually leads to total isolation from the body of Christ and a weakening of their Christian life."

Sometimes I think of all the hurts I've experienced in this ministry, and how they have tended to isolate me. I can remember when a pastor offended me, and refused to support me when I started out in ministry! I invited all the pastors I knew to my wedding. But none of them attended. When it was time to take group pictures, the Master of Ceremonies called out for all pastors to come forward. But there was no one. I was totally rejected by the other ministers in the city.

I remember when a close family friend and neighbour once called me the leader of a cult! I have had trusted pastors betray me and turn against me. I have experienced mid-stream desertion in ministry by trusted people. I have had faithful church members fight against me!

I even decided at a point to stay away from interactions with many people. But, as I thought about this man's toe, I realized what was gradually happening to me. I was being cut off from the rest of the church in Ghana, just like this man's toe. And it was all because of unhealed wounds and hurts. I decided then to allow the wounds in me to heal.

I have noticed that there are many seniors in the ministry who have become disappointed, disillusioned, and unforgiving. I have watched as great ministers who once affected the whole nation, became isolated and cut off themselves from the rest of the body of Christ.

One time I was in the office counselling, when a young man came to me.

He boldly stated, "I have decided to be in your church because I believe this is where God wants me to be."

I queried, "Why did you leave your former church?"

He replied, "I was led by the Spirit to come here."

I asked, "Apart from the Spirit's leading did anything else happen to make you decide to leave that church?"

He hesitated, "Well... there was a slight problem..." And he went on and on about problems that had arisen in his previous church.

I immediately knew that what I suspected was true. This man was hurt, and his unresolved hurts had caused him to be cut off from his church. Christians are often moved away by complicated offences.

Married couples start out with hot, strong and fiery love, which is often blind and unseeing. However, after several years of marriage, many couples either just co-exist and some even hate each other.

How did they retrogress from love to hatred? Often the hurts and offences of marriage were never fully resolved until they were virtually cut off from each other. If Satan can isolate you through hurts, he will have the opportunity to speak to you and trouble you. You see, you are more vulnerable when you are isolated. The book of Hebrews warns us that bitterness can trouble us greatly.

3. Do not be moved by a change in your circumstances.

For David speaketh concerning him, I foresaw the Lord always before my face, for he is on my right hand, THAT I SHOULD NOT BE MOVED:

Acts 2:25

God is with you! God is on your side! You will not be moved by any changes that take place in your life. Because you are unmoveable, you will be a strong Christian.

Unfortunately, the children of Israel hung their harps upon the willows when they encountered their new circumstances. They packed up their instruments of praise because they had been carried away as captives. They said,

...How shall we sing the LORD'S song in a strange land?

Psalm 137:4

Christians who find it difficult to adapt to their new circumstances often weaken in their walk with God. They cannot adapt themselves to their new roles as wives, husbands, mothers, fathers and so on. They are simply unable to adapt themselves to their new jobs, new husbands, new wives, new babies and so on. Sometimes when a Christian relocates to another city, he changes from being a strong and vibrant Christian to being cold and indifferent. He cannot adapt to his new environment.

Why should you turn your back on God because of your new circumstance? Rise up in the name of Jesus! You wanted so much to have a wife, a husband and a job. Now you have it, so adapt quickly to your new circumstance! Marriage can shift you from your calling and your ministry. You must overcome the problems the come with marriage.

...and if thou marry...shall have TROUBLE in the flesh...

1 Corinthians 7:28

It was extremely difficult for me to become a doctor as well as a pastor. When you become a doctor your life changes. Your life becomes totally involved in the condition of your patients. But I had to quickly adapt to my new circumstance in order to continue with the ministry.

You cannot put the Lord aside just because you have travelled to a new country or to a new school. The Christian who cannot adapt quickly to his new circumstances is likely to become weak. You must adapt in order to stay alive!

Learn how to identify these things. Do not be ignorant of the devil's devices. Be strong in the Lord! Be unmoveable! Why fall away now that you know the Lord? God has great plans for you; there is no doubt about it. He has plans to bless you, to prosper you and to increase you in this life. Remember, however, that such blessings are not meant to draw you away from God, but to establish your faith and confidence in Him.

4. Do not be moved from the path of righteousness into short cuts.

...he leadeth me in the paths of righteousness for his name's sake.

Psalm 23:3

Jesus came to die for this world. God so loved the world that He gave His only Son. Satan offered Jesus a short cut to the kingdoms of this world. Satan said, "Bow down and worship me and you will win the kingdoms of this world tonight." 'Again, the devil taketh him up into an exceeding high mountain, and sheweth him all the kingdoms of the world, and the glory of them; And saith unto him, All these things will I give thee, if thou wilt fall down and worship me' (Matthew 4:8-9)

What a quick and easy way for Jesus to accomplish His ministry! Jesus was offered a faster way to save the world. Jesus Christ was too wise to fall for the temptation to take a short cut. Jesus decided to stay on the path of righteousness!

The world is under the delusion that there are short cuts to everything. Unfortunately, some Christians think in the same way. They assume that there must be some short cut to Heaven since there seems to be a short cut to almost everything.

But you cannot escape the cross! Jesus said, "Take up thy cross and follow me." There is no short cut around the cross. You must take up the cross! In this day and age of instant coffee, instant tea and jet travel, everybody wants to have things fast, quick and short.

When I was in boarding school, I learnt the hard way that short cuts must be avoided. Those of us in the junior forms were asked to do some general scrubbing in school. I obtained an excuse duty slip from the doctor. It exempted me from any assigned duties for the next four days. I happened to discuss this excuse duty slip with a friend, and excitedly told him how I wouldn't have to do any hard work for the next four days. Then he came up with what I thought was a bright idea.

He suggested, "Why don't you write "1" before the "4" so it reads "14" days instead of "4"? You will then have fourteen whole days to relax."

As I mused over this suggestion, I thought, "What a good idea! No one will notice." But this friend was the first Judas I was to meet in my life. After I had taken *his* suggestion and changed the '4' to '14', this same friend reported me to the seniors. He told them that I had forged my excuse duty slip.

Everyone pounced on me, and I was charged. I tell you, I suffered greatly for that mistake. First of all, my four days of excuse were cancelled. I was given the most difficult jobs to do. And then I was given extra punishment. From that time I decided: *No more short cuts in life*! I realized long ago that there was no short cut to Heaven. I will have to go the hard way.

We may think that there is a shorter way to Heaven, but there is only one way to Heaven. It is only by accepting the Lord Jesus Christ as your personal Saviour and being born again. There is no short cut.

In the secular world, wise businessmen are wary of any "get-rich-quick" schemes. Many however, are not tired of trying one quick scheme after the other. So they take advantage of every opportunity to make some quick money.

Someone once asked our church to join a new 'get-rich-quick' bank. He explained, "As a growing church you will need a lot of money to help complete your building project." But I immediately said, "It sounds too good to be true, and too quick to be real." So we didn't join it. A few weeks later, I heard of how that new bank had collapsed. Many people lost their money. I also heard of how some churches had lost huge sums of money by saving there.

The Bible says the Kingdom of Heaven is like a mustard seed, which needs time to grow to become a great tree. When you put the seed into the ground, it will need to go through the long process of dying and growing before yielding fruit. Unfortunately, some of us want to escape the processes of dying and growing up. You cannot expect to just put money in the offering and hope that everything will be all right. You cannot avoid the reality of fasting, praying, fellowshipping and witnessing. There are no short cuts in Christianity!

5. Do not be moved by foolish questions.

But foolish and unlearned questions avoid...they do gender strifes.

2 Timothy 2:23

Satan is an expert at throwing questions into the air and creating all sorts of suspicion and confusion. Almost every minister of the gospel is surrounded by suspicion, accusation and questions. God Himself has been accused of not existing. There are men who have risen up to challenge and insult God, thereby confusing the masses. Be careful of foolish questions and above all do not be moved by foolish questions!

Someone once asked, "Who made God?"

Another person said, "I'll come to church if you can tell me whom Cain's wife was".

The answer to this particular question is very simple. But it is a foolish question anyway. You see, the problem is not who married Cain. You just want to find some reason to doubt the authenticity of the Bible! Others would question, "Why are the pastors driving nice cars?" Again, the problem is not with the pastor's car or how much the pastors are being paid. The problem is that you are trying to find some fault with your church. You desperately need to find a reason to justify your actions.

These are foolish questions; a classic symptom of a Christian who is not steadfast. Of course, I am not against the asking of legitimate questions. But there is a difference between a genuine question and a foolish question. Watch out for those who come up with all sorts of criticisms and reviews of the church and its ministers. They often have a hidden motive.

6. Do not be moved to do evil.

AND ALL THE CITY WAS MOVED, and the people ran together: and they took Paul, and drew him out of the temple: and forthwith the doors were shut. And as THEY WENT ABOUT TO KILL HIM, tidings came unto the chief captain of the band, that all Jerusalem was in an uproar.

Acts 21:30-31

Satan is on a campaign to move people into evil. Evil spirits inspired the city to charge on Paul and kill him for his powerful preaching. Be careful that you are not moved to do evil.

You must also be careful that you are not moved to experiment with evil things. Curiosity, they say, killed the cat. But in another sense curiosity also kills many Christians. Some Christians have been deceived by the devil into thinking that they are missing something. They therefore become curious and want to experiment with these forbidden areas.

Some would say, "I haven't tasted alcohol all my life. I want to know what it feels like to be drunk."

Others would say, "I have never used drugs before and I want to know what it feels like to be 'high'." You may only find out what it is like to be mad! You may acquire what we call marijuana-induced schizophrenia.

I was with my boss in a consulting room at the mental hospital one day when a mother brought in her son. This boy had been experimenting with marijuana. The Psychiatrist took this young boy on a tour of the mental hospital. There were men in little cubicles making various strange noises. There were special places for very wild mad men. The Psychiatrist warned this young boy that if he continued experimenting with drugs his curiosity would end him up in this "zoo"! I will never forget that tour.

It is this same kind of curiosity, which led the prodigal son out of his father's house to eat with pigs. What couldn't the prodigal son have had at home? He admitted that his own father's servants had more than enough to eat. He was just curious about what was going on out there.

You will notice men with very beautiful and charming wives, who still chase after other women. Some of these men are just curious. They think there is more to discover. There is nothing new under the sun. There is nothing new to see!

7.   Do not be moved to join murmurers and rebellious people.

Do all things without murmurings and disputings.

Philippians 2:14

Murmuring means to complain, to grumble, to mumble, to criticize and to rebel. There are Christians who murmur at home, at work and in church. God is against those who murmur. He was especially displeased with the people of Israel when they murmured against Him and Moses. Some complained and nagged so much that they never made it to the Promised Land. People who murmur, complain and rebel never make it to the Promised Land. In my experience people who murmur and complain often leave their churches and eventually become weak Christians.

When you complain against someone, it is likely that you are angry with the person or that you don't like that person anymore. Those who complain against their governments are often angry with their government. In the same way those who murmur against the church are often angry with God and are ready to leave Him. Mark those who murmur and complain. They are very moveable. There is one sin that is compared to witchcraft in the Bible. That is the sin of rebellion.

For REBELLION is as [like] the sin of WITCHCRAFT...

1 Samuel 15:23

Rebellion is the fight against all authority. Rebellion often camouflages itself as the fight for independence. Many so-called freedom and independence fighters are actually downright rebels. There are also many rebellious elements in the church. Rebellion stems from the heart. Every rebellious child of God has rejected legitimate authority in his life. I have known Christians who do not want anything, be it human or divine, to instruct them concerning their lives.

It was rebellion against his father's authority that led the prodigal son to leave home. The rebellion in the prodigal son's heart led him to eat with pigs. I am sure you don't want to end up eating with pigs. Don't be a rebel. All rebels are destined to end in one way. Ask the prodigal son, ask Judas, ask Absalom, ask Adonijah, ask Ahithophel, ask Shimei, and ask Lucifer to tell you what happened to them when they rebelled. All those who are moved to become rebellious are headed for the same place – destruction!

CHAPTER 5

How to Be a Spiritual Christian

And I, brethren, could not SPEAK UNTO YOU AS UNTO SPIRITUAL, but as unto carnal, even as unto babes in Christ.

1 Corinthians 3:1

Rememeber that the human being is made up of three parts: spirit, soul and body. Any one of these three parts will dominate you and your entire life. If your flesh dominates you, you are called a fleshly (or carnal) Christian! If your soul dominates you, you are called a soulish Christian! If your spirit dominates you, you are called a spiritual Christian!

It is much better to be a spiritual Christian than a carnal one. It is much better to marry a spiritual Christian than a carnal Christian. It is much easier to live with a spiritual person than a carnal person. A carnal person goes by his feelings and feelings are very fleeting and dangerous to depend on.

You must make every effort to go out of the carnal phase and become a spiritual Christian. When you are spiritual, you are more influenced by spiritual things and your spirit man is more developed. To be spiritually minded is life but to be a carnally minded Christian is dangerous and deadly (Romans 8:6).

The following keys will help you to be a spiritual person. When you are spiritual, people will refer to you as 'that spiritual brother'. It is a good thing when people refer to you as a spiritual person. People have a great respect for spiritual Christians because it is not easy to attain spirituality.

1.   Become a spiritual Christian by praying often.

Prayer will make you a spiritual person. Jesus said, "Pray lest you fall into temptation". Prayer keeps us from falling away from God. Anybody you spend time talking to becomes close to you. In the same way, any Christian who spends time talking to God will become close to Him. It follows that if you don't spend time praying to God, you will be far from Him.

This is how people fall in love with each other. Many of us forget that if you continuously communicate with somebody, he or she becomes close to you. You can unknowingly fall in love with a man or woman who is not your partner. Spending time together with somebody makes you close, whether you intend to be close or not. So when a Christian spends less time praying, he is unknowingly moving away from God. When you pray, God gives you strength to overcome temptations. He will strengthen you to do His will and you will not fall away.

Many years ago, God knew I was going to experience a serious testing of my Christian faith so He woke me up early in the morning to pray. Tongues were flowing out of my spirit like a river and I knew something was amiss, so I prayed the more. I lay down on the floor and continued in prayer. As a young Christian I was normally doing an hour a day in prayer, but this time I prayed for over three hours. And that day I met a strange woman. The Bible tells us about a young man in Proverbs who met a strange woman. I had a similar experience.

And, behold, there met him a woman with the attire of an harlot, and subtil of heart.
Proverbs 7:10

I had no idea what this Christian lady had in mind. But that day, I tell you my friend, God delivered me! I believe my deliverance was very much related to the prayer time I had had in the morning. I was very strong. Where did that spiritual strength come from? Where did the spirituality come from? Jesus told His disciples to pray because they might fall into temptation.

The Lord gave me strength through prayer. If you see a Christian who doesn't pray, you are looking at a Christian who will fall into one temptation after another, until he is destroyed.

2.   Become a spiritual person by seeking the will of God.

And the world passeth away, and the lust thereof: but HE THAT DOETH THE WILL OF GOD ABIDETH FOR EVER.
1 John 2:17

Only spiritual people seek the will of God. People who are not spiritual are not concerned about whether they are in the will of God or not. Doing the will of God is a very clever way of living long and living a blessed life. He that doeth the will of God abideth forever. Staying in the will of God and seeking the will of God are very important for surviving as a Christian.

As a minister I have learnt not to have a strong desire for anything in particular. It can easily destroy your ministry. Mind you, I also have desires, but they are subject to the Word of God in me. The strongest desire in a Christian's life should be for the will of God to prevail.

Do not sacrifice your spirituality for your human desires. A spiritual person will sacrifice his personal desires so that the will of God will be done. Anyone who has a very strong desire for material things is not likely to become a strong spiritual Christian.

3. Become a spiritual Christian by having a good conscience.

Holding faith, and A GOOD CONSCIENCE; which some having put away concerning faith have made shipwreck: Of whom is Hymenaeus and Alexander; whom I have delivered unto Satan, that they may learn not to blaspheme.

1 Timothy 1:19-20

Your conscience is the voice of your human spirit. That gentle nudging is the prodding of your spirit. To be spiritual, you must be very sensitive to the voice of your own spirit. The more you drown the voice of your spirit, the less spiritual you will become. A good conscience is necessary to keep you spiritual. Two church members, Hymenaeus and Alexander, put away faith and a good conscience, and thus, they made shipwreck of their Christian lives. As long as we put our conscience away, we will have the capacity to do greater and greater evil until the day that we forsake God.

The conscience is the voice of that better component of a human being (whether a Christian or non-Christian). It is the conscience of a man that tries to keep him from doing evil. It is important to have a good and strong conscience (inner voice). You can either have a strong conscience or a weak one. Paul, the great apostle, said he had a good conscience. He also revealed

44

that he had always maintained a good conscience, even as an unbeliever.

When our conscience becomes hardened, it is difficult for God to speak to us. I have always tried to have a good conscience, because I know the danger of a hardened conscience. It is this conscience which pricks me everyday and keeps me on course. When your conscience is gone, that element within you that can stop you from going far from God is also gone. You are no longer touched by the anointing, by the Word of God, by the preaching or by the Holy Ghost.

Your conscience is like the palm of your hand. Some of us have soft hands, whilst others have callous ones. Your hands will become hardened, and the softness will go away as you do hard work with your hands. In the same way, your conscience will become hardened as you continue to sin without repenting. When believers become indifferent to the promptings of God, it is a dangerous sign.

A pastor friend of mine whose entire family is saved except for one brother told me his story. He related how his mother had taken his brother to so many Full Gospel breakfast meetings that he had become hardened. He had heard many different testimonies from several speakers but these no longer made an impact on his life. Indeed, he knew when the speaker would make an altar call. He knew what the next item on the programme would be.

Many Christians lie and their consciences do not prick them anymore. Some of them can even invent false stories without batting an eyelid. I have heard of pastors who say they preach best after fornicating. The difference between these pastors and you is just a gradual process of hardening. You become harder and harder as you become used to sin. Then at a point when you sin, you won't be bothered anymore.

You can commit bigger or smaller sins depending on your conscience. If you have a very sensitive conscience, the sins that you can commit will be 'small' ones. But as your conscience becomes more hardened and more worn out, your ability to commit 'wilder' sins grows.

Recently, I sat before a certain rich man, and I said to him, "You must be prepared to meet your God at anytime." He was with two of his wealthy friends. He replied that he was not prepared, but he really didn't care. When you get to the stage where you don't care whether you go to heaven or hell, then you are in danger. Perhaps, when you were younger you cared, but you have become so hardened that you don't care anymore.

Every Christian needs to have a sensitive conscience. Do not get used to sin. Do not get to the stage where you do not care anymore. Be sensitive to the little promptings of the inner voice, so you stay spiritual!

4. Become a spiritual Christian by having regular fellowship.

These be they who separate themselves, sensual, having not the Spirit.

Jude 19

Separation from other Christians is a terrible spiritual mistake. It is people who do not have the Holy Spirit who separate themselves. Your spirituality greatly depends on fellowship. If there is a collection of hot coals in a pot, they stay on fire by stimulating each other. If you take one of the coals out of the pot and separate it, the fire in the separated coal goes down. This is what happens to your spirituality when you are disconnected from fellowship with other equally spiritual Christians. Decide to be a spiritual Christian by having regular fellowship.

Our world is made of unspiritual people who hate God. Almost every interaction with the world depletes you and lowers your spirituality. There is no way you can maintain a spiritual life without continuous fellowship. That is why we are urged to go to church and not forsake fellowship. "Not forsaking the assembling of ourselves together, as the manner of some is; but exhorting one another: and so much the more, as ye see the day approaching" (Hebrews 10:25).

5. Become a spiritual Christian by not keeping company with sinners.

Make no friendship with an angry man; and with a furious man thou shalt not go: LEST THOU LEARN HIS WAYS, and get a snare to thy soul.

Proverbs 22:24-25

Whoever you associate with will have an impact on you! The Bible warns us to avoid the company of angry people, lest we learn their ways. The reality is that you are always learning something from whom you are with. "Do not be deceived: Bad company corrupts good morals" (1 Corinthians 15:33).

Your spirituality is greatly compromised when you move around with unspiritual people. Unspiritual people even make fun of spiritual Christians. Unspiritual people give you names and make you feel that you are overdoing things in your quest to be spiritual. You will then feel uneasy when you want to pray or even refer to a scripture.

I once fellowshipped with a brother who made me feel bad for sharing scriptures with him. He told somebody that I had spent the afternoon preaching to him. I was amazed at his description of my normal conversation. A spiritual person will always speak about God and mention scripture. If the people you are with make you feel uneasy for reading your Bible or referring to it, you are with the wrong group. If the people you are with make you feel bad for praying so long, then you are with the wrong group.

6. Become a spiritual Christian by walking in truth.

Stand therefore, having your loins girt about with truth...

Ephesians 6:14

The belt of truth is an integral part of your spiritual armour. Truth is a major part of your spirituality. A spiritual person is a truthful person. Every time you tell a lie you remove part of your spiritual protection and thereby become less spiritual.

To maintain your spirituality you must walk in truth. The apostle John was so happy when his spiritual children lived and walked in truth.

I have no greater joy than to hear that my children walk in truth.

3 John 1:4

Lies are a principal characteristic of Satan. Satan is a liar and the father of all lies. Any time you walk in deception and lying, you are walking into Satan's domain. Many Christians toy with lying. Lying is so common with Christians because many Christians accommodate devils without knowing.

Ye are of your father the devil, and the lusts of your father ye will do. He was a murderer from the beginning, and abode not in the truth, because there is no truth in him. When he speaketh a lie, he speaketh of his own: for he is a liar, and the father of it.

John 8:44

My parents taught me never to tell lies and I think it is one of the greatest and spiritual treasures that they imparted to me. My mother kept telling me throughout my childhood that my father didn't tell lies, so I was not supposed to tell lies. As I grew up I found it difficult to tell lies. Liars are in the same category as wicked people who shed innocent blood. 'These six things doth the Lord hate...a proud look, a lying tongue, and hands that shed innocent blood' (Proverbs 6:16-17).

There are born again Christians who habitually lie through their teeth. They lie to God and to man without batting an eyelid. Many people also do not like the truth. They avoid people who speak plainly and truthfully about issues. Jesus was not popular in the religious community and amongst the Jews because He spoke plainly and truthfully about the hypocrisies and deceptions of our human life. This belt of truth holds the whole armour together. Truth, honesty and sincerity are things that hold your entire Christian life together. Without sincerity your Christian life will disintegrate.

I remember being in a service once with some other brethren. There was a young lady who had been prophesying and holding up the whole service for periods of time. She would stand up whilst the leader was preaching, and interrupt the service with very long prophecies. She would command the priest to stop the administration of communion. This young girl would prophesy and make the entire congregation kneel down and stand up at will.

Many of the leaders were inexperienced, and didn't know what to do. So they would stand back as this young lady dominated the entire service. I had been told about this young lady who had been controlling the meetings, but had never seen her myself. That day, I realized that I was seeing the manifestation of an evil spirit. This young lady stood up and began to take over the service with her prophecies just as had been described to me. So I got out of my seat, took a couple of brothers with me, and escorted her into the basement of the building. I knew that an evil spirit was controlling this young lady. As soon as we got into the basement, this young lady's eyes widened and blazed.

She looked straight at me and said, "Do not quench the Spirit!" I could virtually see the demons dancing in her eyes. This almost unsettled me as I wondered, *"Was I quenching the Holy Spirit?"* Then I said, "You foul spirit, in the name of Jesus. I command you to stop your activities and come out of this girl."

She immediately went into all sorts of writhing movements. The spirit began to manifest, spoke to us using the girl's voice and said many things. I cannot give all the details of this deliverance episode in this book. However, there was one thing that struck me, which I want to highlight here.

I asked the demon spirit, "How did you come into this lady?"

That spirit said, *"The belt of truth was loose."*

The demons had gained access to this young girl's life because the protective armour of truth, sincerity and honesty was deficient in one way or the other. I cannot tell you how exactly this girl's belt of truth was loosed. That is not important to you. What is important is your belt of truth.

Are you honest? Are you sincere? When you make a mistake do you admit it easily? Are you truthful to yourself and to God? I tell you, there are many people who lie to themselves continually and tell themselves, "I am okay", when they know they are not. Do not deceive yourself! Be honest and sincere! Be straightforward! Jesus said, "You will know the truth and the truth will make you free." Don't be angry when you hear the truth. It is the truth that you need.

CHAPTER 6

How to Become a Holy Christian

Follow peace with all men, and HOLINESS, WITHOUT
WHICH NO MAN SHALL SEE THE LORD
                                              Hebrews 12:14

Holiness is a very important attribute that you must develop in your quest to become a strong Christian. To be holy is to be special. God wants holiness in the sense that he wants us to be special and separated unto him.

By living your life in a certain way and not doing what everyone else is doing, you become special, separated and unique in the eyes of the Lord. Don't you want to be special in the eyes of the Lord?

In order to be used by God, you must be separate, different and special. A vessel in the hands of God is a special vessel indeed. Being holy is simply being a special and unusual vessel in the hands of the Lord.

Today, many do not like the topic of holiness because most of us are falling short of the standards in the Bible. However, it will serve you well to strive for holiness! No matter how many times you fall, you must get up again and keep pursuing the high standards of holiness God has set for his people. A righteous man falleth seven times and rises again. Remember, it is worth doing anything and suffering any inconvenience in order for God to choose you and use you.

I want to simplify your search for holiness by giving you what is called the holiness code. The Holiness Code is a term which refers to the set of instructions given in Leviticus Chapters 17 to 26. In this small section of the Bible, the word 'holy' appears forty-three times. The text in this section seems to have a lot to do with holiness. The Holiness Code consists of the following rules which must serve as a guide to your quest for holiness. You must strive to follow the rules in the Holiness Code. You are likely to fail, but the holiness code will be a guide for your attempt at holy living.

THE HOLINESS CODE

Holiness Code No.1: **Keep all the commandments of God.**

If ye walk in my statutes, and keep my commandments, and do them; then I will give you rain in due season, and the land shall yield her increase, and the trees of the field shall yield their fruit.

Leviticus 26:3-4

Holiness Code No.2: **Fear and respect your father and your mother.**

Ye shall fear every man his mother, and his father, and keep my sabbaths: I am the Lord your God.

Leviticus 19:3

Holiness Code No.3: **Do not worship idols.**

Turn ye not unto idols, nor make to yourselves molten gods: I am the Lord your God.

Leviticus 19:4

Holiness Code No.4: **Remember the poor in your midst.**

And thou shalt not glean thy vineyard, neither shalt thou gather every grape of thy vineyard; thou shalt leave them for the poor and stranger: I am the Lord your God.

Leviticus 19:10

Holiness Code No.5: **Do not steal.**

Ye shall not steal, neither deal falsely, neither lie one to another.

Leviticus 19:11

Holiness Code No.6: Do not tell lies and deceive people.

Ye shall not steal, neither deal falsely, neither lie one to another.

Leviticus 19:11

Holiness Code No.7: Do not use God's name in vain.

And ye shall not swear by my name falsely, neither shalt thou profane the name of thy God: I am the Lord.

Leviticus 19:12

Holiness Code No.8: Do not cheat someone of his wages nor hold on to it.

Thou shalt not defraud thy neighbour, neither rob him: the wages of him that is hired shall not abide with thee all night until the morning.

Leviticus 19:13

Holiness Code No.9: Be kind and considerate towards the handicapped and never harm them.

Thou shalt not curse the deaf, nor put a stumblingblock before the blind, but shalt fear thy God: I am the Lord.

Leviticus 19:14

Holiness Code No.10: Ensure that there is justice and fairness towards all men no matter how rich or poor they are.

Ye shall do no unrighteousness in judgment: thou shalt not respect the person of the poor, nor honour the person of the mighty: but in righteousness shalt thou judge thy neighbour.

Leviticus 19:15

Holiness Code No.11: Do not spread rumours or bad stories.

Thou shalt not go up and down as a talebearer among thy people: neither shalt thou stand against the blood of thy neighbour: I am the Lord.

Leviticus 19:16

Holiness Code No.12: Do not hate your brother in your heart or bear someone a grudge.

Thou shalt not hate thy brother in thine heart: thou shalt in any wise rebuke thy neighbour, and not suffer sin upon him. Thou shalt not avenge, nor bear any grudge against the children of thy people, but thou shalt love thy neighbour as thyself: I am the Lord.

Leviticus 19:17-18

Holiness Code No.13: Do not practice sorcery or divination.

Ye shall not eat any thing with the blood: neither shall ye use enchantment, nor observe times....Regard not them that have familiar spirits, neither seek after wizards, to be defiled by them: I am the Lord your God.

Leviticus 19:26, 31

Holiness Code No.14: Do not let your daughters become prostitutes and sexually cheap girls.

Do not prostitute thy daughter, to cause her to be a whore; lest the land fall to whoredom, and the land become full of wickedness.

Leviticus 19:29

Holiness Code No.15: Keep the Sabbath and show respect to the house of God.

Ye shall keep my sabbaths, and reverence my sanctuary: I am the Lord.

Leviticus 19:30

Holiness Code No.16: Honour the aged.

You shall rise up before the grayheaded and honor the aged, and you shall revere your God; I am the Lord.

Leviticus 19:32 (NASB)

Holiness Code No.17: Give strangers fair treatment and show them kindness.

And if a stranger sojourn with thee in your land, ye shall not vex him. But the stranger that dwelleth with you shall be unto you as one born among you, and thou shalt love him as thyself; for ye were strangers in the land of Egypt: I am the Lord your God.

Leviticus 19:33-34

Holiness Code No.18: Do not be cheat or dupe people in business.

Ye shall do no unrighteousness in judgment, in meteyard, in weight, or in measure. Just balances, just weights, a just ephah, and a just hin, shall ye have: I am the Lord your God, which brought you out of the land of Egypt.

Leviticus 19:35-36

Holiness Code No.19: Do not give your children over to idols and demons.

Again, thou shalt say to the children of Israel, Whosoever he be of the children of Israel, or of the strangers that sojourn in Israel, that giveth any of his seed unto Molech; he shall surely be put to death: the people of the land shall stone him with stones.

Leviticus 20:2

Holiness Code No.20: Do not make tattoos and marks on your body.

Ye shall not make any cuttings in your flesh for the dead, nor print any marks upon you: I am the Lord.

Leviticus 19:28

Holiness Code No.21: Do not commit adultery.

And the man that committeth adultery with another man's wife, even he that committeth adultery with his neighbour's wife, the adulterer and the adulteress shall surely be put to death.

Leviticus 20:10

Holiness Code No.22: Do not engage in homosexuality.

If a man also lie with mankind, as he lieth with a woman, both of them have committed an abomination: they shall surely be put to death; their blood shall be upon them.

Leviticus 20:13

Holiness Code No.23: Do not have sex with animals.

If And if a man lie with a beast, he shall surely be put to death: and ye shall slay the beast. And if a woman approach unto any beast, and lie down thereto, thou shalt kill the woman, and the beast: they shall surely be put to death; their blood shall be upon them.

Leviticus 20:15-16

Neither shalt thou lie with any beast to defile thyself therewith: neither shall any woman stand before a beast to lie down thereto: it is confusion.

Leviticus 18:23

Holiness Code No.24: Do not have sex with your sister or step sister.

The nakedness of thy sister, the daughter of thy father, or daughter of thy mother, whether she be born at home, or born abroad, even their nakedness thou shalt not uncover.

Leviticus 18:9

And if a man shall take his sister, his father's daughter, or his mother's daughter, and see her nakedness, and she see his nakedness; it is a wicked thing; and they shall be cut off in the sight of their people: he hath uncovered his sister's nakedness; he shall bear his iniquity.

Leviticus 20:17

Holiness Code No.25: Do not have sexual relations with a woman as well as her daughter.

Thou shalt not uncover the nakedness of a woman and her daughter, neither shalt thou take her son's daughter, or her daughter's daughter, to uncover her nakedness; for they are her near kinswomen: it is wickedness..

Leviticus 18:17

Holiness Code No.26: Do not have sexual relations with your grandchild.

The nakedness of thy son's daughter, or of thy daughter's daughter, even their nakedness thou shalt not uncover: for theirs is thine own nakedness.

Leviticus 18:10

Holiness Code No.27: Do not have sexual relations with your mother or your step mother.

And the man that lieth with his father's wife hath uncovered his father's nakedness: both of them shall surely be put to death; their blood shall be upon them.

Leviticus 20:11

Holiness Code No.28: Do not have sexual relations with your aunties and uncles.

Thou shalt not uncover the nakedness of thy father's sister: she is thy father's near kinswoman. Thou shalt not uncover the nakedness of thy mother's sister: for she is thy mother's near kinswoman.

Thou shalt not uncover the nakedness of thy father's brother, thou shalt not approach to his wife: she is thine aunt

Leviticus 18:12-14

Holiness Code No.29: Do not have sexual relations with your brother's wife or your son's wife

Thou shalt not uncover the nakedness of thy daughter in law: she is thy son's wife; thou shalt not uncover her nakedness. Thou shalt not uncover the nakedness of thy brother's wife: it is thy brother's nakedness.

Leviticus 18:15, 16

Holiness Code No.30: Do not have sex with your maid.

And whosoever lieth carnally with a woman, that is a bondmaid, betrothed to an husband, and not at all redeemed, nor freedom given her; she shall be scourged; they shall not be put to death, because she was not free.

Leviticus 19:20

CHAPTER 7

How to Become a Mature Christian

THAT WE HENCEFORTH BE NO MORE CHILDREN, tossed to and fro, and carried about with every wind of doctrine, by the sleight of men, and cunning craftiness, whereby they lie in wait to deceive.

Ephesians 4:14

There are three types of Christians: babies, children and mature Christians. When you are a baby Christian, you are easily hurt, always crying and heavily dependent on others. A baby cannot control his flesh and eases himself anywhere at any time.

Children on the other hand are a little more controlled in their flesh, but are unstable, unable to sit down and always running all over the place. Children bear little fruit and contribute little to the building of the home. Indeed, children are expensive to have and practically make the house dirtier and untidy. Children are also unstable because they do not know much about anything. They do not know why and how food is set on the table. They do not know how and why babies are born. They do not even know or understand when there are conflicts in the home. They believe every story; even the most fantastic and unbelievable ideas are believed and trusted by children.

Knowledge, understanding and wisdom are the hallmarks of maturity. When someone is becoming a mature Christian, he moves quickly from the state of ignorance and naivety. He knows why, he knows what, he knows where and he knows when things have to be done.

To be a mature Christian, you must know why things are done. You must have the reasons for all Christian practices. You must not just do something because everyone does it. You must do things because you know the reasons for them. I want to share with you thirty things that Christians do and the reasons why they do them.

If you know the answer to these questions, you will be well on your way to becoming a mature Christian. The reason why a Christian does something is because the Bible says so. The word of God is the guide for all Christian behaviour. Through the word of God, you will be thoroughly furnished for every good work. 'All scripture is given by inspiration of God, and is profitable for doctrine, for reproof, for correction, for instruction in righteousness: that the man of God may be perfect, throughly furnished unto all good works' (2 Timothy 3:16-17).

If you know the reasons why things are done it means you are not just following the crowd. It means you are maturing in your faith. You must have a scripture to back every answer you give. If you do not have scriptures to back your answers you are not stable or rooted in the Lord.

Thirty Questions and Answers for Mature Christians

1. **Why are Christians different from unbelievers?** Because the Bible describes us as a peculiar people.

   Just as the Jews are different and odd in every community where they are found, we should be different wherever we are. Christians are to look different, behave differently, go to different places and do different things. Christians are supposed to be odd, peculiar, unusual, strange and different. Why is this? The reason is in the Bible. Read it for yourself.

   > Who gave himself for us, that he might redeem us from all iniquity, and purify unto himself A PECULIAR PEOPLE, zealous of good works.
   >
   > Titus 2:14

2. **Why do Christians not have close friendships with unbelievers?** Because the Bible says we are not to be unequally yoked to unbelievers. Christians are different from unbelievers. Christians are called righteousness whilst unbelievers are called unrighteousness.

   > BE YE NOT UNEQUALLY YOKED TOGETHER WITH UNBELIEVERS: for what fellowship hath righteousness with unrighteousness? And what communion hath light with darkness? And what concord hath Christ with Belial? Or what part hath he that believeth with an infidel?
   >
   > 2 Corinthians 6:14-15

3. Why do Christians have to be friendly to unbelievers? Because the Bible teaches us to reach out to all men. We have been instructed to reach out to the world. The Bible teaches us to go into the world and teach all kinds of people.

Go ye therefore, and TEACH ALL NATIONS, baptizing them in the name of the Father, and of the Son, and of the Holy Ghost.

Matthew 28:19

4. Why do Christians not marry unbelievers? Because the Bible says we should not be unequally yoked to unbelievers. Just as an ox cannot be yoked with a cat to do a good work on a farm, a Christian cannot be joined with an unbeliever in marriage.

Be ye not unequally yoked together with unbelievers: for what fellowship hath righteousness with unrighteousness? And what communion hath light with darkness? And what concord hath Christ with Belial? Or what part hath he that believeth with an infidel?

2 Corinthians 6:14-15

5. Why do Christians not go to beach parties, drink-ups, unbeliever parties and night clubs? Because the Bible says that all things are lawful but not all things are helpful. It will not help you to be holy in your Christian life if you are found at parties and night clubs. You will find yourself drinking, taking drugs and having sex casually with the next available person.

All things are lawful for me, but all things are not expedient: all things are lawful for me, but ALL THINGS EDIFY NOT.

1 Corinthians 10:23

6. **Why do Christians not commit fornication?** Because the Bible teaches that we should not have sex before marriage. The Bible is clear on our sexual behaviour. The Bible contains a lot of guidelines for our sexual conduct.

    For this is the will of God, even your sanctification, that YE SHOULD ABSTAIN FROM FORNICATION.

    1 Thessalonians 4:3

7. **Why do Christians not watch pornography?** Because the Bible teaches us to abstain from all appearances of evil. Pornography is an evil thing which is destroying many lives. It may not be mentioned in the Bible because it was recently invented. A simple scripture clearly warns us to abstain from appearances of evil.

    Abstain from all appearance of evil.

    1 Thessalonians 5:22

8. **Why do Christians speak in tongues?** Because the Bible teaches that when you speak in tongues you are speaking to God Himself. Also, when you speak in tongues you edify yourself and build yourself up. Don't you want to be built up as a Christian? Don't you want to be stronger? Don't you want to be on fire for God? If you do want any of these things, you will know that speaking in tongues is a great key for your spiritual development.

    For HE THAT SPEAKETH IN AN UNKNOWN TONGUE SPEAKETH NOT UNTO MEN, BUT UNTO GOD: for no man understandeth him; howbeit in the spirit he speaketh mysteries.... He that speaketh in an unknown tongue edifieth himself .

    1 Corinthians 14:2, 4

9. **Why do Christians not listen to unbelievers' music?** Because the Bible teaches that evil spirits can be drawn into your life by listening to the wrong kind of music. Evil spirits can also be driven away by the right kind of music as you

see in the scripture below. Even music without words, like David playing on the harp, has power to drive away evil spirits. There is no neutral music. Music either has a positive spiritual effect or a negative one.

...Behold now, an evil spirit from God troubleth thee. Let our lord now command thy servants, which are before thee, to seek out a man, who is a cunning player on an harp: and it shall come to pass, when the evil spirit from God is upon thee, THAT HE SHALL PLAY WITH HIS HAND, AND THOU SHALT BE WELL.

1 Samuel 16:15-16

And it came to pass, when the evil spirit from God was upon Saul, that David took an harp, and played with his hand: so Saul was refreshed, and was well, and the evil spirit departed from him.

1 Samuel 16:23

And Elisha said, As the Lord of hosts liveth, before whom I stand, surely, were it not that I regard the presence of Jehoshaphat the king of Judah, I would not look toward thee, nor see thee. But now bring me a minstrel. And it came to pass, when the minstrel played, that the hand of the Lord came upon him.

2 Kings 3:14-15

10. **Why do Christians have long, rather than short relationships unto marriage?** The church is the bride and Jesus is the bridegroom. Jesus is having a long relationship of two thousand years with His bride before marrying us. He is ensuring that we become a glorious church before He finally commits to the marriage. He is a wise bridegroom. Are you a wise bride?

For this cause shall a man leave his father and mother, and shall be joined unto his wife, and they two shall be one flesh. This is a great mystery: but I SPEAK CONCERNING CHRIST AND THE CHURCH.

Ephesians 5:31-32

11. Why do Christian girls not expose their bodies? Because the Bible teaches that Christians should not act unbecomingly! Christian girls dress decently without exposing their breasts and other body parts unnecessarily. Christian girls are like this because they do not want to act in an unbecoming, inappropriate way.

...DOES NOT ACT UNBECOMINGLY; it does not seek its own, is not provoked, does not take into account a wrong suffered.

1 Corinthians 13:5 (NASB)

12. Why do Christian girls not over-emphasize dressing and make-up? Because the Bible teaches that Christians should rather beautify the inner man. Christian girls are more concerned about the hidden person of the heart. Christian girls are more concerned about the inner qualities they must develop, rather than the hairstyles they must have. Christian girls are aware that really good brothers are attracted to inner qualities more than the outward.

Do not let your adornment be merely outward – arranging the hair, wearing gold, or putting on fine apparel – rather let it be the hidden person of the heart, with the incorruptible beauty of a gentle and quiet spirit, which is very precious in the sight of God.

1 Peter 3:3-4 (NKJV)

13. Why do Christian girls look nice? Because the Bible teaches that our body is the temple of God. Christian girls dress nicely because they know that their bodies are the temple of God. They know that God lives in them. A nice house usually has a nice person living in it. Christian girls know that it is important to have a nice house to give a good impression about God who lives in them.

Know ye not that ye are the temple of God, and that the Spirit of God dwelleth in you?

1 Corinthians 3:16

14. Why do Christians not steal or cheat in examinations?
Because the Bible says we should steal no more. Christians
are born again and changed people. They no longer do the
things they used to do. They do many things differently.
They know the scripture that warns us not to steal any more.
This is why we can sing the song, *"The things I used to do, I
do them no more"*.

Let him that stole STEAL NO MORE: but rather let him
labour, working with his hands the thing which is good,
that he may have to give to him that needeth.

Ephesians 4:28

**15. Why do Christians not swear, curse, insult or use vulgar
words?** Because the Bible says no corrupt communication
should proceed out of your mouth. Christians know what the
Bible says about how we speak. Christians cannot speak in
the same way as non-Christians.

Let no corrupt communication proceed out of your mouth,
but that which is good to the use of edifying, that it may
minister grace unto the hearers.

Ephesians 4:29

16. Why do Christians tell the truth? Because the Bible says
we should put away lying. Christians know that lying is an
evil thing and they are not going to have anything to do with
it.

Wherefore PUTTING AWAY LYING, speak every man
truth with his neighbour: for we are members one of
another.

Ephesians 4:25

**17. Why do Christians try to remain virgins till they get
married?** A Christian's sexual life is controlled by the word
of God. Because the Bible says fornication should not happen
even once, Christians remain as virgins till they get married.

But fornication, and all uncleanness, or covetousness, let it not be once named among you, as becometh saints.

Ephesians 5:3

18. Why do Christians witness and talk about Jesus Christ? Christians know that they have been commanded to reach out to the whole world. Because Jesus said we would be witnesses when the Holy Spirit came upon us, Christians witness when they are inspired by the Holy Spirit. A lack of the Holy Spirit is reflected in the witnessing practices of a Christian.

But ye shall receive power, after that the Holy Ghost is come upon you: and YE SHALL BE WITNESSES unto me both in Jerusalem, and in all Judaea, and in Samaria, and unto the uttermost part of the earth.

Acts 1:8

19. Why must Christians sacrifice and suffer for Christ? Christians know that suffering is part of Christianity. The Bible tells us to take up our cross and follow Jesus. Because of this, Christians are ready to suffer and sacrifice for Jesus Christ.

And whosoever doth not bear his cross, and come after me, cannot be my disciple.

Luke 14:27

20. Why are Christians happy people who have fun? The kingdom of God is righteousness, peace and joy in the Holy Ghost. Because of this, Christians are full of righteousness, joy and peace.

For THE KINGDOM OF GOD IS not meat and drink; but RIGHTEOUSNESS, and PEACE, and JOY IN THE HOLY GHOST.

Romans 14:17

21. Why must Christians do well in exams? Because Christians must have a good report from outsiders, all Christians want to do well in school.

Moreover HE MUST HAVE A GOOD REPORT OF THEM WHICH ARE WITHOUT; lest he fall into reproach and the snare of the devil.

1 Timothy 3:7

22. Why must Christians forgive others? Christians know that their own prayers will be hindered if they do not forgive others. Christians are therefore very concerned that they forgive others for their sins.

And when ye stand praying, forgive, if ye have ought against any: that your Father also which is in heaven may forgive you your trespasses. But IF YE DO NOT FORGIVE, NEITHER WILL YOUR FATHER WHICH IS IN HEAVEN FORGIVE YOUR TRESPASSES.

Mark 11:25-26

23. Why must Christians be open to each other? Because the Bible teaches us to confess our faults one to another and pray for one another. Christians are open to each other and share their difficulties readily.

Confess your faults one to another, and pray one for another, that ye may be healed. The effectual fervent prayer of a righteous man availeth much.

James 5:16

24. Why do Christians lead a quiet life and mind their own business? Leading a quiet life and minding your own business is a direct command in the Bible.

And to MAKE IT YOUR AMBITION TO LEAD A QUIET LIFE and ATTEND TO YOUR OWN BUSINESS and work with your hands, just as we commanded you.

1 Thessalonians 4:11 (NASB)

25. Why do Christians not stay angry for a long time? Christians do not stay angry for long because we are not to let the sun go down on our anger. This means that the maximum time for being angry will be twelve hours. Christians do not maintain quarrels for days, weeks and years as unbelievers do.

Be ye angry, and sin not: let not the sun go down upon your wrath

Ephesians 4:26

26. Why do Christians read their Bibles everyday? Christians depend on the word of God for everything. The Bible teaches that man shall not live by bread alone but by every word that comes out of the mouth of God.

But he answered and said, it is written, Man shall not live by bread alone, but by every word that proceedeth out of the mouth of God.

Matthew 4:4

27. Why do Christians pray everyday? Because the Bible teaches us to pray without ceasing. To pray without ceasing is to pray every day, every hour and every minute. It is the most natural thing for Christians to pray every day because we are told to pray without ceasing.

Pray without ceasing.

1 Thessalonians 5:17

28. Why do Christians respect prophecies and preaching? Christians respect prophecies because the Bible clearly teaches us to not despise prophesying.

Quench not the Spirit. Despise not prophesyings.

1 Thessalonians 5:19-20

29. Why do Christian women learn how to cook and do household chores? Because the Bible teaches younger women to guide the home. Guiding the home involves cooking, cleaning, looking after husbands. All good Christian ladies want to be able to guide the home.

I will therefore that the younger women marry, bear children, GUIDE THE HOUSE, give none occasion to the adversary to speak reproachfully.

1 Timothy 5:14

30. Why do Christians listen to their pastors? Because the Bible teaches us to obey those who watch over our souls. Pastors are seen as people who watch out for the souls of their members.

Obey them that have the rule over you, and submit yourselves: for they watch for your souls, as they that must give account, that they may do it with joy, and not with grief: for that is unprofitable for you.

Hebrews 13:17

CHAPTER 8

How You Can be a Zealous Christian

But IT IS GOOD TO BE ZEALOUSLY AFFECTED ALWAYS in a good thing, and not only when I am present with you.

Galatians 4:18

Your zeal shows how much you are on fire for God. Your zeal is an indicator of your strength in the Lord. When you are on fire, you are far from being cold. You must become zealous because it is a good thing to be zealously affected always. Jesus Christ was zealous! Paul was zealous! You can be zealous too! If you belong to Christ, then go all the way and become zealously affected for Jesus Christ. Here are some keys that will help you to become a zealous Christian.

And because iniquity shall abound, the love of many shall wax COLD.

Matthew 24:12

To be zealous is to be on fire for God. There is nothing cool about a zealous person. Some Christians are very 'cool' in the house of the Lord. They refuse to be part of jubilant praise and worship. They don't join in shouting or clapping their hands to the Lord. They just refuse to release themselves in the presence of the Lord.

If you want God to be attracted to you, then be like King David. David lost all his inhibitions when he danced before the Lord. There was no coolness about the way he danced. In fact, he danced until his clothes fell off!

A man without zeal has no joy! To such a man, it is a bother to lift up his hands to the Lord or shout with the voice of triumph. It is amazing that this same "cool" Christian would lose his 'coolness' when his favourite soccer team is playing. He will shout, scream and clap his hands when a goal is scored.

When Christians are losing their zeal, they become aloof, diplomatic and uninterested. They yawn, look bored and keep glancing at their watches during the service. But there is nothing cool about a zealous person!

1. **Be zealous by not comparing yourself with other Christians.**

    For we dare not make ourselves of the number, or compare ourselves with some that commend themselves: but they measuring themselves by

themselves, and COMPARING THEMSELVES AMONG THEMSELVES, ARE NOT WISE.

2 Corinthians 10:12

Most Christians are not zealous! If you compare yourself with the average Christian you will only live a mediocre, lukewarm Christian life. You will also think you are okay because everyone is like that. When you get to heaven you will be shocked because you compared yourself with the wrong people.

We always try to find out who else is like us. When we are down, we instinctively want to take others with us. Like drowning men, we want to pull others down to be where we are.

Do not take confidence in the fact that others seem to be doing as badly as you are. That is a false assurance because every man shall bear his own burden. You can tell when people are trying to reassure themselves.

A friend once told me about an incident that jolted him into becoming a Christian. He told me, "I was a party-going, night-life person with lots of girlfriends. One day, I was going home in a friend's car after one of our usual parties when I noticed that the car was unusually quiet. So I decided to slot in some music to liven up the atmosphere. I picked up one of the CDs lying in the front of the car and inserted it. To my utmost surprise, instead of music, there was preaching."

I exclaimed, "Hey, what's this? Since when did you start listening to such things? Are you also one of those born again people?"

And his friend replied, "Hey, I am securing myself."

He then realised: "If our car were to have an accident and both of us were to die, my friend may have gone to heaven and I to hell." His friend had secretly been building himself up spiritually.

You see, people are secretly seeking God and securing their places in heaven. You better make sure that you are doing the right thing. Do not look at what others are doing. You are born alone, and you will die alone. Do not even look to your husband or your wife. It is unusual for husbands and wives to be born on the same day. It is even more unusual for them to die on the same day. You will stand before God as an individual. Never forget that fact of life. Do not compare yourself with others if you want to be a zealous Christian!

2. Be zealous by focusing on the soon-coming Christ.

Focusing on the soon return of Jesus Christ will make you zealous for Him. The world is truly amused when we say that Christ is coming soon. They think it is a theory cooked up by some deranged people. Some Christians believe that the Second Coming of Christ is a reality but they do not expect it to happen soon; at least, not in their lifetime. They suppose they can enjoy themselves and forget about the coming of Christ. But what you are forgetting is that Christ's coming will be a very *unexpected* event.

...the day of the Lord so cometh AS A THIEF IN THE NIGHT. For when they shall say, Peace and safety; then sudden destruction cometh upon them, as travail upon a woman with child; and they shall not escape.

1 Thessalonians 5:2-3

A pregnant woman can go into labour suddenly. Everything may be all right today but the very next day may be filled with chaos. That is how the coming of the Lord will be.

Jesus compared his coming to the coming of a thief. No one expects a thief. I remember years ago when thieves broke into my father's house. We were not expecting anything of the sort, but it just happened. The whole world will be very surprised when Jesus comes again. Many have taken God's grace period of repentance for granted.

You may be planning to have your grand wedding. But it may never come on. Perhaps, those who are in school may never complete their courses. The trumpet will suddenly sound, and those of us who are washed in the blood of the Lamb, and ready for the Saviour will be caught up in the clouds to be with Him forever. Focus on this great event of the rapture and you will be a very zealous Christian.

3. Be zealous by believing that you can die at any time.

And he said, This will I do: I will pull down my barns, and build greater; and there will I bestow all my fruits and my goods. And I will say to my soul, Soul, thou hast much goods laid up for many years; take thine ease, eat, drink, and be merry. But God said unto him, Thou fool, THIS NIGHT THY SOUL SHALL BE REQUIRED OF THEE: then whose shall those things be, which thou hast provided?

Luke 12:18-20

You will be a zealous Christian if you think about death. Many people serve God in a lukewarm way because they think they will not see Him in the near future. 'I have many years ahead of me' they say. 'I have many years to catch up with any lost time.' People think that because they are young they still have a lot of time. Also they think they have enough of their lives ahead of them to sort things out with God.

The whole world stood in shock at the news of the death of people like Princess Diana. No one in his wildest imagination would have thought that someone so young, so charming and so beautiful could be taken off the face of the earth so suddenly. The security of an armour-plated Mercedes Benz with airbags all around could not prevent her death in a car accident in Paris.

Everyone thinks that there is more time. I'm sure Princess Diana thought there were many more years ahead. We all did! But it was not so. That is why the whole world trembled with shock. It is not safe to assume that there is more time. The Bible warns us that because we don't know the day or the hour Christ will come, we must be ready all the time. The key word here is preparation and readiness.

...thus will I do unto thee...because I will do this unto thee...PREPARE to meet thy God...

Amos 4:12

Jesus told us the story of a man who had a successful business. He had so much that he wondered what to do with the profits. He decided to build bigger barns to store his goods. In our time this would be equivalent to opening new bank accounts.

When he completed his projects, he said to himself, "Soul, thou hast much goods laid up for many years. Take thine ease, eat, drink and be merry." God reacted immediately from Heaven and said, "...This night thy soul shall be required of thee." In other words, I want to have a discussion with you tonight. God has the right to call you up for a discussion at any time. God is showing us here that there is just a step between us and death.

There are three times in your life when people will gather to honour you. They gather when you are born and christened. Then they gather again when you are getting married. And finally, they will definitely also gather for you when you die. Somebody might contend that he or she is too young to die. But go to the mortuary, and you will discover that even little babies die.

Do not cool down because you think you are still young and there is more time. You never know when God will summon you to account for your life. It is time to be zealous for the Lord. You will have all of eternity to rejoice in the Lord and celebrate. You must show yourself to be zealously affected always in a good thing.

4. Be zealous by fasting often.

Then shall thy light break forth as the morning, and thine HEALTH shall spring forth speedily... Then shalt thou call, and the Lord shall answer: thou shalt cry, and he shall say, Here I am...
Isaiah 58:8-9

Fasting is not an option if you want to be a zealous Christian. Jesus said in Matthew 6:16: "when ye fast..." He didn't say, "if you fast." This means that He expects us to fast. Fasting has its rewards. In Isaiah 58, God has listed some of the rewards of fasting.

One of the rewards of fasting is that you will stay spiritually healthy. Fasting is a spiritual exercise that keeps us on our toes. The more you fast, the more spiritual energy you generate. The more you fast, the more spiritually tuned up you will be.

Fasting makes a believer zealous. In the Bible the word associated with fasting is affliction. In fact, the word affliction can be interchanged for fasting.

Wherefore have we FASTED...wherefore have we AFFLICTED our soul...

Isaiah 58:3

Be AFFLICTED, and mourn, and weep...

James 4:9

Before I was AFFLICTED I went astray: but now have I kept thy word.

Psalm 119:67

How do you afflict yourself? According to the psalmist, one way you can afflict yourself is by fasting. He said that before he fasted he went astray, but when he fasted, he was able to keep God's Word and stay on track. Then in Psalm 119:71, he says, "It is good for me that I have been afflicted, that I might learn thy statutes." Do you think that God is saying it is good to have sickness and disease? Affliction in that sense is not sickness. In this context God is saying that it is good for the Christian to fast.

Fasting helps you to be humble. In James 4:10, the Word of God says, "Humble yourselves in the sight of God and He will lift you up." When the psalmist fasted in Psalm 35:13, he said, "I humbled my soul with fasting". Carrying your pastor's Bible, speaking softly, or walking slowly are not signs of humility. God says you can humble yourself by fasting.

During a fast, especially when you have not eaten for several days, you experience extreme weakness in your body. This kind of suffering in the flesh sobers you. It makes you humble. And if there is anything we need in this modern age of Christianity, it is humility. Remember that pride comes before a fall, and fasting will take away the pride that leads many to a fall. As a believer you need to fast, so that you will be filled with the zeal of the Lord.

You will be able to walk in zealous Christianity because many spiritual problems will be solved through your life of frequent fasting. Some people have problems that will dampen their zeal. Some of these problems that kill your zeal must be solved through fasting.

...THIS KIND goeth not out but by prayer and FASTING.

Matthew 17:21

Not all problems are the same. Some difficult ones can be solved only through fasting. It is no wonder that Christians who do not fast are weighed down by all kinds of problems. Even winter should not prevent Christians from fasting. I have heard Christians in Europe and America complain that it is not possible to fast during the winter. It is possible. During several of my church-planting exercises, I have had to fast during the winter.

I remember a brother who could not believe that I was fasting in the winter. He asked me, "How can you fast when it is so cold?" He explained that eating helps to keep warm. We can fast in the winter. We can fast when we are young and we can fast when we are old. The prophet Daniel fasted when he was eighty years old. Fasting is the greatest key to zealous Christianity.

5. Be zealous by not forgetting what God has done for you.

God warned the children of Israel...AND THOU FORGET the Lord...which brought thee forth...

Deuteronomy 8:14

Christians become more zealous when they remember how kind God has been to them. A young lady who is selected out of hundreds of girls in the congregation is full of zeal to be a good wife, as long as she remembers how blessed she was to be chosen. When she forgets where she came from she becomes like Vashti and loses her zeal to please her husband. Don't ever forget that it is Christ who brought you into your position, and blessed you.

Many of us have forgotten who we used to be. We have forgotten what it was like to have a hangover in the morning. Let us remember where the Lord brought us from. When we bought our first church building, we were all so excited. We marched from the Korle-Bu Hospital in Accra, to our new headquarters location, amidst singing and dancing. The building was an old cinema that we had rebuilt into a beautiful cathedral. Indeed, we played before the Lord. Somebody who watched me later on video laughed and commented: "It seems that old cinema hall meant a lot to you". I replied, "You don't know where the Lord has brought me from. I have not forgotten, and I do not intend to forget."

Many churches have forgotten the vision and principles of their founders. They have forgotten the ideals and standards that their founding fathers stood for. That is why many of them are in a backslidden condition. If some founders of churches were to rise from the dead now, they would not associate with the very churches they founded.

I always try to remember why I came into the ministry. Why did I leave the respected and noble practice of medicine to come into the often controversial and ridiculed job of being a pastor? My original motivation was to win souls. I try to keep that at the forefront of my mind and I keep pressing on to win more souls. If I forget why I came into the ministry, I may slide into education, medicine, social work or even politics.

Andrae Crouch's famous song, 'How can I say thanks' sums it all up. You cannot do much for the Lord. How can you really say thanks? Your gratitude to the Lord must only inspire you to be zealously affected always!

CHAPTER 9

How to Become a Fruitful Christian

Ye have not chosen me, but I HAVE CHOSEN YOU, AND ORDAINED YOU, THAT YE SHOULD GO AND BRING FORTH FRUIT, and that your fruit should remain: that whatsoever ye shall ask of the Father in my name, he may give it you.

John 15:16

Every Christian should aim to be fruitful. This is why Christ saved us. He saved us so that we would go forth and bear fruit to his glory. God is glorified when we bear much fruit. God has chosen you and ordained you already. Your ordination is an ordination onto fruitfulness. These are the keys that will make you fruitful.

1. Become fruitful by having spiritual goals.

That ye might walk worthy of the Lord unto all pleasing, BEING FRUITFUL IN EVERY GOOD WORK, and increasing in the knowledge of God.

Colossians 1:10

It is important that you have great ambitions to do something for God with your life. Do not just be happy to be a Christian. You must aim higher. You must have the goal of doing something for God.

As a believer if you don't go forward, you will go backwards. If you don't have an ambition to press forward in Christ, you will have a problem. Christians who have no spiritual ambition have the tendency to become fruitless. Paul had a vision to keep pressing on.

...but this one thing I do, forgetting those things which are behind...I PRESS toward the mark for the prize of the high calling...

Philippians 3:13, 14

We must forget the good and the bad and press on ahead. We have all had good and bad experiences in our lifetime. But we must forget about them and press forward. Some Christians are hooked on to the past. They tell tales of the great exploits God used them to do in the past. You cannot just be content with what happened some years ago. What about the present? What is God using you to do today? The time to minister to others is now.

For when for THE TIME YE OUGHT TO BE TEACHERS, ye have need that one teach you again...

Hebrews 5:12

You must have spiritual goals and these will propel you to rise up to minister to others. The greatest blessing you can have is to become a blessing to others. God promised Abraham that He would bless him so much that he would become a blessing to others.

There was a time in my life when I couldn't preach. But I did not stay there. I knelt down before a mature Christian brother and asked him to lay hands on me so I would be able to preach. After that prayer I started preaching. I stood before little groups and began ministering to them.

Maybe you also have the same problem. Maybe you feel shy to speak in public. Act in faith by speaking the Word with a few people, and you will be surprised at what God can do.

A Christian should have the ambition to be useful in God's house. Many people do not wish to be great in God's house. Instead, many Christians crave to be millionaires. They look for all the opportunities to be great in the secular world. When it comes to the things of God, many Christians have no energy.

When God called me, I wanted to be a good preacher. I listened to and watched other preachers minister. I invested both time and money to achieve my goal of being fruitful. You must have some ambition in the house of the Lord. You must have the ambition to be fruitful.

2. Do not allow riches to quench your fruitfulness.

...and the deceitfulness of riches...choke the word, and it becometh unfruitful.

Mark 4:19

Rich Christians are some of the most fruitless Christians on earth. They think their money can buy their way into the mansions of heaven. As people become more successful, they tend to stay away from church. When the Lord blesses you, do not make the mistake of allowing the responsibilities associated with the new blessings to choke the Word.

Remember that it was God who gave you the power to acquire wealth. God, by blessing you, did not intend to keep you away from Him! You rarely see the so-called "big-shots" at prayer meetings and crusades. They do not turn up for all night prayer meetings probably because they are tired from all the work they do. Some people think they can do something more profitable rather than spending their time in church.

Learn how to maintain the glow in spite of your newfound treasures. Don't allow your riches to crowd out the Lord!

3. Do not allow the cares of the world to kill your fruitfulness.

And the cares of this world...choke the word, and it becometh unfruitful.

Mark 4:19

Jesus told the story of a sower who went out to sow. Some seeds fell on the wayside, some on stony ground, some among thorns and the rest on good ground.

Jesus compared the four types of ground to four types of hearts. In one heart, thorns choked the word. In another, the heart was like a stone, so that the Word could not enter. In another heart, the Word fell by the wayside. It was only the good heart that bore fruit. This story implies that only about a quarter of all those who hear the Word of God will eventually remain in Christ and be fruitful.

The thorns are the cares of the world which choke the word of God and the message of the Holy Spirit. So what are the cares of the world?

Paying your debts, paying your bills, and all the responsibilities that go with family life fall under these "cares". There is nothing wrong with paying your bills or looking after your family. Indeed, if you have a wife or family, you ought to look after them. A husband's duty is to fellowship with his wife and to take care of his children. These are legitimate challenges that every one in this world will have to grapple with. But God warns us against becoming over burdened with these responsibilities. These cares should not dominate our lives. When they begin to dominate your life, they will kill your fruitfulness.

When Christians take on new jobs, they become so engrossed in them - to the detriment of their spiritual lives. Sometimes because of such new jobs, they neither go to church nor have their quiet times any more. Every student's "care" is to pass his examinations but God should not be excluded from your life because of your books. As a medical student I successfully combined my schoolwork with my pastoral work. For years I was a student as well as a pastor.

I never put the work of God aside because of school. In my ministry, I have had medical students pastoring large branches of the church faithfully. It is not an impossible task. As a medical student, I often asked, "Is being a medical student a curse? Does it mean that I cannot serve God anymore?" The answer is No! Being a medical student is just another 'care' of this world which must not be allowed to choke God's Word and work.

A new baby or a pregnancy should not prevent you from bearing fruit. Other Christians have made it, and so can you! When our first son was born, I carried him to church when he was only seven days old. I had a preaching appointment to honour, and had to go with my wife and my newborn son. I remember how we carried our seven-day-old baby through the cold weather onto the buses, and in the streets in order to keep this preaching appointment in Geneva. My baby didn't die. Neither will yours, if you continue to do the work of the Lord. Rise up and be fruitful in spite of all the cares and responsibilities of the world.

4. Do not be lazy if you want to be fruitful.

The slothful man saith, There is a lion without, I shall be slain in the streets.

Proverbs 22:13

The lazy Christian is full of amazing excuses. A lazy Christian will say that he cannot leave his bed because of an imaginary lion in the street. Such a person will not amount to much because anyone who wants to be successful must be prepared to work hard!

When I was in Achimota School I passed with distinction at the ordinary level exams. It didn't just happen. I had to work very hard! While some of the students were playing around, I was studying very hard. In the third year of my medical schooling I earned another distinction. In preparation for that exam, I didn't sleep in the night for six weeks. I slept in the afternoons between 2p.m. and 6p.m. Then from 6p.m. till the next day at 2p.m., I wouldn't sleep. I would go for walks, memorizing and retaining some of the course material. I remember walking up and down in the 'R' Block of the medical students' hostel, memorizing all sorts of information about worms, flies, and insects: this worm lays so many eggs per minute, that insect flies at this speed per second, it dives at this angle into the water, etc. When other students were asleep, I was walking behind their rooms memorizing things about worms, crabs, scorpions and every other creature I had to learn about. Success comes with diligence.

Seest thou a man diligent in his business? He shall stand before kings; he shall not stand before mean men.

Proverbs 22:29

Those who are doing well are not practicing any kind of magic. Their success comes from hard work. In the same way, fruitful Christians are not just miraculously bearing fruit. They are working hard at their Christian lives!

I have pastors who work very hard and often leave the church very late. There are also unpaid volunteers who make great sacrifices of time. It is this great commitment that makes the church work.

Laziness will not take anybody to Heaven. Seest thou a man who is slothful? He can easily go to Hell! It takes hard work to bear fruit. Watch the lazy Christians in the church; they never become fruitful Christians.

5. Develop the highest type of commitment if you want to be fruitful.

It is only when you are highly committed to someone that you can marry the person. Through the highest level of commitment, you will enter into marriage and have children. Indeed, only the highest level of commitment produces fruit. When a man is married to a woman, because they are committed to each other for life, they are able to open up their private parts to each other and interact at that level. It is that deep level of interaction that leads to the creation of children. Deep commitment is always necessary for fruitfulness.

Deep commitment is necessary if you want to become a fruitful Christian. Consider your level of commitment now. Are you committed to the church and the work of God? Or are you just visiting? It is only the deeply committed Christians who bear fruit in a church. There are countless Christians who are just visiting churches, but are not committed to any of them. If they don't feel too happy with the pastor or his sermons, they will move to the next church.

God expects the believer to be like a tree that is planted by the rivers of water. The rivers of water are the powerful, life-changing messages that flow from the pulpit every Sunday. Every Christian must be planted in the house of the Lord. You must have somebody to relate to as your pastor. God created us as sheep who need a shepherd. You need to belong somewhere!

I remember one friend who finally came home to Africa after sojourning in Europe for sometime. He didn't want to join this church or that church. He was just not committed anywhere.

He would go here today and there tomorrow. At a point I had to remind him that according to the Book of Job, it is the devil who goes 'to and fro'. Stability and commitment are important for fruitfulness. Fruitfulness is only possible with the highest level of commitment.

6. Be fruitful by avoiding bad company.

...bad company ruins good morals.

1 Corinthians 15:33

Amongst Christians there is always bad company. The worst kind of company is that of Christians who do not bear fruit and who do nothing for God. Bad company is a very bad symptom, with a very poor prognosis. Fruitless barren Christians move together in bands and swarms of aimless money-loving people. Bad company will eventually lead you to bad places. When you see a Christian who has bad friends, it is likely he will become just like his friends.

There is a saying: "Birds of the same feather flock together." "Show me your friend, and I will show you your character!" We can tell the kind of person you are by just looking at the kind of friends you have!

Within every large church there are smaller groups of Christians. When you observe these groups, you will discover that they are people with the same kind of "feather". The friends you move with will either lead you to church or to bad places.

If you are a real believer and you want to remain in Christ, then you need to have good friends. They should be real born-again Christians, who attend a "born-again" church. They must believe the things you believe. You must go to church together. Your friends must not have anything against your going to church. If they do, they must not be your friends!

The person you marry will keep you company for the rest of your life, and this 'marital company' will truly affect you. King Solomon, who built the temple and accomplished great things for the Lord, eventually fell from the Lord. His wives turned his heart away from God. Solomon's wives were bad company for him!

You do not need to expose yourself to the circumstances of bad company. You are not more anointed than Solomon. If the Bible warns that bad company can ruin your life, you'd better believe it and save yourself! Every wife affects her husband, and every husband has great influence over his wife. Whoever you are, your wife will influence the way you think. If your husband thinks in a certain way, in the process of time, you will eventually think in the same way. If your wife does not want you to be in the ministry, you will not be in the ministry. I know this from experience. If my wife had opposed my going into the ministry, I don't think I would have been able to come this far. It is time to choose the right company. It is time to make friends with fruitful people. It is time to make friends with those who are doing something for God.

CHAPTER 10

How to be Ready to Meet God

...prepare to meet thy God...

Amos 4:12

A strong Christian is ready to meet God. I spoke with a flight attendant on a flight from Johannesburg to Accra. I asked her if she was scared because of the many plane crashes we were hearing about.

She quietly answered, "You know, I am scared."

Then I asked her, "Are you ready to meet God?"

She said, "No, I am not. I do not think I have lived enough." Then she asked me, "Are you ready to meet God?"

I said, "Yes, I am." She was taken aback.

"Really?" she said.

I told her, "You can only be ready through the blood of Jesus who died for you."

A strong Christian is ready to meet God at any time. There are two events that will make you meet God. There are two events that you must be ready for: the rapture of the saints and your death. Both of these events will be the end of your life on this earth. A good Christian must be ready for the coming of the Lord. A good Christian must also be ready to die.

Be Ready for the Rapture

For the Lord Himself will descend from heaven with a shout, with the voice of the archangel and with the trumpet of God, and the dead in Christ will rise first. Then we who are alive and remain will be caught up together with them in the clouds to meet the Lord in the air, and so we shall always be with the Lord. Therefore comfort one another with these words.

1 Thessalonians 4:16-18

The rapture is when Jesus Christ will come for all Christians. We will be caught up in the clouds and be carried into heaven by the Lord. Will you be ready for the coming of the Lord or will you be left behind? You must be ready for the Lord when He calls for you. No one knows the day or the hour when he will be called by God. The rapture is an event that the church has waited for, for many years. Definitely, at the time when we think not, Jesus will come again and we will be caught away. All through the Bible, there are warnings to be ready. Be a strong Christian and be ready for the coming of the Lord!

Then saith he to his servants, THE WEDDING IS READY, but they which were bidden were not worthy.

Matthew 22:8

THEREFORE BE YE ALSO READY: for in such an hour as ye think not the Son of man cometh.

Matthew 24:44

You may have been a strong Christian before. You may have been a strong Christian when you were in school. Perhaps you have backslidden and changed completely. You may have even been a minister of the gospel. Today, there is no sign of your former zeal, steadfastness, holiness and spirituality. That is a very dangerous thing because you must be ready *in the moment* the Lord appears.

Many years ago, I was a medical student in the University of Ghana. We had to catch a bus to the hospital every day at 7.00am. This was a special bus that took medical students from the university campus to the hospital, which was an hour's journey away.

One morning, my roommate and I were late and we missed the bus. We ran to the other side of the campus hoping to catch it from there, but we missed it by a few seconds. We could not believe that we were being left behind. We stood there sweating and panting, holding our white coats, our bag of skeletal bones and our medical books. How dejected and disappointed we were! We were medical students. *We were qualified* to be on the bus, but *we were simply not ready* at the moment the bus came by. I never forgot that lesson and I never missed the bus again!

You see, you may be qualified to go to heaven. But you must also be ready for the moment that Jesus comes for us. There were ten virgins that Jesus spoke about. Indeed, they were all virgins. They were all clothed in white. They all had lamps and they all had oil at a point. But at the time that the bridegroom came, some of them were simply not ready. Jesus warns us not to be like the foolish virgins who were not ready when the bridegroom came.

Be Ready for Death

Another event you must be ready for is death. Will you be ready to die if the Lord calls you? Remember that immediately after death comes judgment. There are two ways to die. You can die the death of a righteous man or you can die the death of a wicked unbeliever. If you live the life of a strong Christian you will end well and die the death of a righteous man.

> ... Let me die the DEATH OF THE RIGHTEOUS, and let my last end be like his!
>
> Numbers 23:10

How do you want your end to be? Do you want to grow stronger and stronger until the last day? You can choose to be steadfast, faithful, unmovable, spiritual, fruitful and mature. You can die the death of a righteous man. That is the right way for you to go! That is the will of God!

We will all stand before the presence of God to account for our lives. When that time comes and you are ushered into the presence of God, what will you say? Will you be ready? Would you have done what God wanted you to do?

A Christian brother was committing fornication when he heard a loud blast. He thought it was the sound of the trumpet heralding the return of Christ. So he jumped out of the bed, but was not caught up to heaven. He was so worried, because he thought that he had been left behind at the rapture. This anxious Christian was overreacting to the honk of a big bus. It is important to be ready for the coming of the Lord or for your own death when the Lord calls you.

The Death of the Righteous

Jesus Christ died on the cross for the sins of the whole world. He was a righteous person and had done no evil. His last words revealed the kind of person who was dying on the cross. He said, 'Father, forgive them for they know not what they do.' In His last moments on this earth he was full of forgiveness and mercy for wicked murderers.

He also said to John, 'Look after my mother' and to his mother, 'Look after John.' He acted responsibly even though He was facing imminent death. His very last words were, 'it is finished.' He had finished His ministry.

Will you have finished your ministry in the day of your death? Will you have accomplished all that God has for you? The only way to die the death of a righteous person is to fulfil your ministry. When you have done all that God wants you to do you will go out of this world in peace saying, 'It is finished!'

A famous missionary to Burma who laboured tirelessly for many years fell ill at the age of sixty-one. Adoniram Judson, an American missionary to Burma, had married for the third time, having lost two previous wives through illness. His last wife, Emily, was only in her twenties when she married him.

After only two years of marriage, Adoniram had caught a severe cold and a high fever. The illness settled in his chest and dysentery followed. Adoniram spent the next few months in bed, trying to recover, as his wife tenderly nursed him.

One day he exclaimed to his wife, "I have gained the victory at last. I love every one of Christ's redeemed, as I believe He would have me love them. And now I lie at peace with all the world and what is better still, at peace with my own conscience."

But steadily, Adoniram grew worse and his doctors insisted that his only hope of survival was to go on a sea voyage so that he would benefit from the fresh ocean winds. His wife Emily, apprehensively booked Adoniram on the French ship *Aristide Marie.* She could not accompany him because she was only three weeks away from giving birth to her second child. Obviously, it would not be a good idea to give birth on a ship. Adoniram went on this fateful journey but unfortunately did not make it to America. After only six days into the journey he died on the ship. Because the ship was far from any shore he was buried at sea. Three weeks after his departure his wife Emily gave birth to a son. She did not hear about his death until three months later. In those days, there was very little fast communication. When she heard of his death on the ship, she packed her belongings and went back to America.

But before sailing on the ship Adoniram had told Emily some great and memorable words which inspire me greatly. As he prepared to go on board the ship for that fateful voyage, he confided in his beloved wife, Emily. I have presented his last few words in five italicised statements. I have also presented a little explanation of these powerful statements of a great man who died the death of a righteous man. The great tireless missionary said:

1. *I AM NOT TIRED OF MY WORK!:* I am not tired of the work that God has given me to do on this earth. I am not tired of preaching. I am not tired of people. I am not tired of counselling. I am not tired of people. I am not tired of travelling. I am not tired of witnessing.

2. *I AM NOT TIRED OF THE WORLD!:* I am not tired of the difficulties, the suffering and the painfulness that God has allowed me to endure in this world. I am not tired of the struggle that there is in this world.

3. *IF CHRIST CALLS ME HOME I SHALL GO WITH THE GLADNESS OF A BOY BOUNDING AWAY FROM SCHOOL!:* I will always be excited at the thought of dying and meeting my Saviour face to face. I am ready to go to heaven at any time. I am ready to die with joy. I am excited at the prospect of going to heaven.

4. *DEATH WILL NEVER TAKE ME BY SURPRISE!:* I am ready for death at any time, any day. Going out of this world will never be a shock, surprise or disappointment to me. I have laboured, I have finished, I have accomplished what He sent me here to do.

5. *I FEEL SO STRONG IN CHRIST!:* Even though I am facing a life-threatening situation, I feel strong, blessed and encouraged in the Lord. My current difficulties have not taken away my spiritual strength and zeal for the Lord.

The Death of the Wicked

When you are not a strong Christian, you will be frightened by the prospect of death. This is only natural because you are not ready to meet with God. More than once, I have been called by people who were dying and were afraid to meet with God.

On one occasion, I received a call to see a man who was dying in hospital. This man was not strong in the Lord. I had tried to talk to this man earlier about Christ. But when I spoke to him, he was angry and even threatened me. He shut me up and told me that I had no right to talk to him about God. He made it clear to me that I should mind my own business and not be over-righteous in thinking that others were not born again.

Yet, when he was dying in hospital, he had people call me frantically, "Please come quickly to the hospital". He was terrified because in his last few hours he began to see creatures and beings standing around his bed. He told his assistant, 'they are coming for me. Can't you see them, they are coming for me.' He spent his last few days and hours in terror as these creatures gathered around to take him away. Before I was able to get to him, I had a call that he was dead.

It is important to serve the Lord and be a strong Christian who is ready to die and meet God at any time. Paul said, 'For me, to live is Christ and to die is gain.' Dying was not a frightening prospect for the great apostle. Paul said, 'I have run my race. I have finished my ministry. I have fulfilled my call. I am ready to meet my God.' Are you ready to meet your God?

Dear Christian friend, I have shared with you many things that will help you to be strong in the Lord. ***BECOMING A CHRISTIAN IS NOT ENOUGH. YOU MUST BECOME A STRONG CHRISTIAN.*** Decide now to live your life for Jesus. Decide now to be a mature, spiritual, holy and strong believer.

It is a great thing to serve the Lord. It is nicer to be a strong Christian than a weak Christian. You will have much more fun, joy and excitement in the Lord, as you become a strong believer.

Then shall ye return, and discern between the righteous and the wicked, between him that serveth God and him that serveth him not.

Malachi 3:18

To the making of many books there is no end...